HERITAGE GARDENS

The World's Great Gardens Saved by Restoration

GEORGE PLUMPTRE

HERITAGE GARDENS

The World's Great Gardens Saved by Restoration

MITCHELL BEAZLEY

For my mother, who restored our family's garden.

HERITAGE GARDENS
George Plumptre

First published in Great Britain in 2007
by Mitchell Beazley, an imprint of
Octopus Publishing Group Limited,
2–4 Heron Quays, London E14 4JP.

ISBN 978 1 84533 271 6

A CIP catalogue record for this book is available from
the British Library.

Set in Bembo

Colour reproduction in Singapore by Sang Choy
Printed and bound in China by Toppan Printing Company Ltd.

Commissioning Editor: Helen Griffin
Senior Editors: Peter Taylor and Leanne Bryan
Art Editor: Victoria Burley
Design: Sarah Rock
Editor: Sarah Zadoorian
Picture Research Manager: Giulia Hetherington
Production: Lucy Carter

PREVIOUS PAGE
Autumnal avenues of replanted lime trees in the Grosser
Garten, Herrenhausen, Germany.

RIGHT
Weigela florida "Variegata" in flower beside the ditch at
East Lambrook Manor, Somerset, England.

CONTENTS

6   FOREWORD

8   WHY RESTORE GARDENS?

38   THE ART OF RESTORATION

66   ICONS OF THEIR AGE

90   HEALING TIME

122 DESIGNERS & PLANTSMEN

154 POSTWAR RESTORATIONS

188 GENUINE, NOT PASTICHE

202 GAZETTEER OF GARDENS

203 BIOGRAPHIES

205 BIBLIOGRAPHY

206 INDEX

208 ACKNOWLEDGMENTS

BELOW
The restored stone
arch at Arkadia,
Lowicz, Poland.

Foreword

One of my first assignments as a young garden journalist was to attend the press preview in 1979 of the newly restored National Trust garden at Claremont in Surrey, England. We were led around the garden by senior National Trust gardens adviser Graham Stuart Thomas, who explained, as we took the well-worn circuit, that this magical capsule of eighteenth-century English garden history had been lost for almost 100 years. Neglect and enthusiastic Victorian planting of rhododendrons and other invasive shrubs had destroyed a seminal early landscape moulded by four of the "greats" of the English Landscape movement: Sir John Vanbrugh, Charles Bridgeman, William Kent, and Lancelot "Capability" Brown.

The most exciting and memorable moment came when we reached Bridgeman's grass amphitheatre; a unique feature in eighteenth-century gardens, but one that had completely disappeared. The curving terraces had been painstakingly rebuilt using the evidence of contemporary illustrations and descriptions. Most evocative and decorative of all the contemporary illustrations of the eighteenth-century gardens are a series of views painted in oils by a brilliant but anonymous artist of the time who has been given the glorious name of the "Master of the Tumbled Chairs", after a curious series of tipped-over chairs that appear in his Claremont views. His set of paintings provided vital evidence for the trust's restoration.

Ever since that day I have admired and been fascinated by garden restoration projects and appreciated the amount they contribute to our knowledge and understanding of garden history. Over almost 30 years I have also become aware of the different motives for restoration and the circumstances under which they take place, and this book is an attempt to bring together the extraordinary range of examples from different countries. Garden restoration took place in the past to some degree, but to a great extent it is only since the beginning of the twentieth century that it has assumed increasing importance and acceptance. In the nineteenth century (and, indeed, into the next), many commentators, historians, and designers supported the view that gardens evolve naturally, and if a once great garden had declined into a state of natural decay and slumber, so be it. To stop the clock and attempt to recreate something that dated from centuries earlier would produce something unrealistic and superficial.

Since then, attitudes have changed dramatically, encouraged by certain events and by an increasing reverence for the past and a strong sense of the need to preserve it. While many contemporary garden-makers have looked to the future during the last century, others have looked back: sometimes fondly, sometimes with concern to preserve something that might be lost. This has ensured that the work of gardeners and designers who are particularly admired – Gertrude Jekyll in England, Beatrix Farrand in the United States, or Lawrence Johnston in France – is identified for restoration and then preservation. Equally, it has ensured that styles of gardening that fell out of fashion and were swept away – as were the seventeenth-century formal garden and the High Victorian garden in England – have been restored to preserve lasting examples of garden styles that threatened to disappear.

One brutal influence since the early twentieth century has been war, which was responsible for the destruction of many great gardens around the world, especially in Europe and Russia during World War II. There is a fierce incentive for restoration once peace has been re-established. And in the increasing awareness of the need for conservation in its broadest sense, outstanding gardens around the world have been identified if at risk of neglect, decline or destruction, and in many cases saved by intervention. In England, the National Trust has led the way since the 1960s with a series of ambitious, meticulous restorations; in the United States, the Garden Conservancy is widespread, while the decision by UNESCO to register World Heritage Sites has provided the most significant international safety net and ensured the survival of gardens in danger, from Shalimar Bagh in Lahore, Pakistan, to Lednice in Poland.

Those involved in garden restorations have found the projects absorbing and often intensely moving. There are constant references to "waking sleeping beauties" and a sense that a long-neglected garden that is discovered and identified for restoration should be treated with respect. It is this which often means the initial reaction when a newly restored garden is revealed can be critical of gleaming newness despite the fact that it will only ever be temporary. Written accounts of different restoration projects: at Aberglasney in Wales, Heligan in England, Serre de la Madone in France, and The Mount in the United States, all clearly portray these different influences and considerations.

The debate about the merits of garden restoration will never go away. Nor should it, because any restoration project should be carried out to the highest-possible standard. Of course, archaeology and technology, together with exhaustive research, have ensured that the techniques available today are formidable. To return to Claremont, the fact that features of one of England's most significant landscape gardens and examples of work by the movement's leading exponents have been restored from a state of terminal decay is a source of fascination and should be applauded. It should be the reaction to all garden restoration carried out to the necessary standard.

George Plumptre

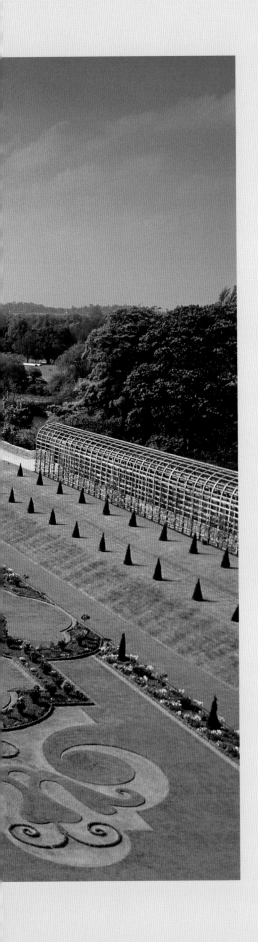

WHY RESTORE GARDENS?

Garden restoration has not always met with approval. As Ernest de Ganay, the distinguished French garden historian, commented in the 1940s on the vanished seventeenth-century garden of Château d'Harcourt, "The past, once gone, must be the past" (Mosset and Teyssot, 1991: 525). During the last 50 years, however, many factors have lent support to the principle of garden restoration. The justification for individual restorations varies by case, some being historically important or rare survivals, while others preserve the work of a renowned designer or repair wartime damage.

There is no single overriding incentive behind the many different types of garden restoration illustrated in the chapters that follow – other than, perhaps, a growing sense that important gardens should be restored for their own intrinsic value, and, in an age when conservation as a wider theme is so prevalent, the wish to preserve as much evidence of our gardening past as possible. Equally variable are the practical challenges faced by individual restoration projects and the degree to which they attempt to produce an accurate replica of the original garden. In some cases, as at the royal garden of Het Loo in the Netherlands, the restoration delves into minute detail in order to reinstate gardens whose original symmetrical arrangement make accuracy of pre-eminent importance. Elsewhere, in gardens restored because of their associations with an admired individual, the priority has more often been to preserve the place in the spirit of its creator. Lawrence Johnston's garden in the South of France, Serre de la Madone, is a good example of this approach (see page 46).

A spectacular variety of gardens has been brought back to life from utter dereliction, or been restored to a period original by removing the "overlay" of later periods. In many cases, these have been long-term projects requiring enormous financial resources. Restorations carried out early in the twentieth century were able to use the evidence of historic descriptions and illustrations to restore lost layouts, and had available the craft skills needed to rebuild temples or repair statues. However, technical developments in the second half of the twentieth century have opened up the possibility of a more precise, in-depth approach. Soil analysis, surveying, and archaeology have, for instance, assisted the work at Stan Hywet Hall in America (see page 104). Some recent projects have taken advantage of the ever more sophisticated techniques at their disposal.

The approach to the restoration of planting has also become far more meticulous. When England's National Trust restores a period garden such as the late seventeenth-century Westbury Court, it restricts the varieties used to those known to have been in cultivation at the time. At Upton Grey, also in England, owner Rosamund Wallinger scoured nurseries for the exact plants shown in Gertrude Jekyll's planting plans for the Arts and Crafts garden (a search that took years; see page 124), while at Montgomery Place in America (see page 110), the plant notebooks that Violetta Delafield kept in 1921–49 yielded the evidence required for replanting her schemes with accuracy.

As reflected by the contents of this book, the majority of restorations have taken place since the 1940s. But others, such as Château de Courances and Château de Vaux-le-Vicomte in France, where work was carried out in the nineteenth

century, demonstrate that the desire to restore gardens is not new. Restoration as an endeavour has a history of its own, and ours is not the only generation to feel passionate about past periods of garden style. Courances and Vaux-le-Vicomte were both sponsored by wealthy private owners, although most of the gardens described here have either been restored by a public body or with some degree of public participation.

While the garden at Mount Vernon in the United States was recreated as a tribute to George Washington, the country's first president, the Italian Villa d'Este was revived as an icon of the Italian Renaissance. Other restorations have been precipitated by a surge of local feeling for a threatened garden, as at Carmen de los Martires in Spain. This is but a sample of the great range of motives for restoration represented in the pages that follow; whatever the individual reasons behind each of these gardens, their new status is to be applauded. It has sometimes been suggested that turning the clock back interferes with the very nature of gardens, which is to change over time, but imagine the loss to garden history if none of the gardens described here had been restored. Taken together, they surely enrich our understanding of the past.

PETERHOF

Some of the most ambitious projects have been those where national pride is a motivating force. Where this is inspired by the desire to overcome wartime damage, and the garden is in the hands of the state, the results are often dramatic. Perhaps the most impressive example of this type is Peterhof, the most famous of the series of imperial Russian gardens located near St Petersburg. It must rank as one of the most symbolic, ambitious, and flamboyant in the history of restoration. The work was symbolic because, like the palace that overlooks it, the garden was reduced to rubble during World War II; it was ambitious because of the scale of the garden; and flamboyant because the original boasted a dazzling array of ornaments, including ranks of gilded statues and numerous dramatic fountains. Having been created by Peter the Great, the founder of modern Russia, Peterhof was also the palace that most potently embodied Russia's imperial past.

The garden at Peterhof was first laid out in 1714, with the central axis running from the palace to the edge of a natural terrace overlooking the Gulf of Finland. Water tumbles down a double cascade below the palace, collecting in a central pool

OPPOSITE
The long canal at Peterhof leads from Peter the Great's summer palace towards the sea. The building and its park, begun in 1714, symbolized Russia's victory over Sweden and its domination of the Gulf of Finland.

RIGHT
Peterhof's marble cascade and gilded statues were restored from total ruin after the end of World War II. Before work started, 35,000 mines and booby traps left by the occupying German forces had to be removed.

dominated by a vast statue of Samson prizing open the jaws of a lion; beyond this, the axis continues towards the sea along a long central canal lined with fountains and trees. The origin of Peterhof's importance as a symbol of national pride is indicated by the location, grandeur, and iconography of the garden. It was created to celebrate Peter the Great's victory over Sweden in the Great Northern War of 1700–21.

After the fall of the imperial regime that had built Peterhof, the palace and garden continued to be strongly associated with a sense of cultural identity. The long German occupation during World War II was viewed by Russians with anger and dismay. Marina Tikhomirova was chief custodian of Peterhof before the war, and when she returned to the area a few days after it had been liberated in January 1944, she found a scene of incredible chaos: "ruins half-covered in snow, an enormous anti-tank trench cutting through the whole garden and beyond it the burnt-out ruins of the Great Palace ... dark-red against the dazzlingly white snow. But that was only the start of the tragic discoveries on a day that sticks in the memory" (Hayden, 2005: 37).

Restoration began almost immediately, but only after some 35,000 mines and booby traps left by the Germans had been removed. Of the smashed or stolen statues that had to be reconstructed, most challenging was the great 3m (10ft) figure of Samson. It was reproduced by sculptor Vasily Simonov with the aid of photographs provided in response to a public appeal. The new bronze figure was completed in August 1947. A few weeks later, thousands arrived at Peterhof to mark the moment the fountains were turned back on. "Two miles away a rocket was fired to signal that the sluice had been opened in the restored water system and shortly afterwards a column of water shot triumphantly from the mouth of the lion to the immense satisfaction of all present." (Hayden, 2005: 38).

LEFT
As this view towards the palace suggests, the postwar restoration of Peterhof's vast and flamboyant landscape was one of the most ambitious ever carried out in the history of garden restoration.

WESTBURY COURT

While Peterhof is an exceptional garden, a cultural icon whose restoration by the Soviet state helped revive national pride in postwar Russia, the work of the National Trust in England presents quite a different picture. A major force in garden restoration since the 1960s, the National Trust has led the way in its approach to fund-raising and in the painstaking, historical accuracy of its work. One of their least-known but most atmospheric gardens, Westbury Court, is hidden away on the west side of the river Severn in Gloucestershire. It has the distinction of being the trust's first major restoration and it set the standard for all future projects. Of particular interest is the way the trust set out the terms of the restoration: to preserve a small but extremely rare historical garden in a threatened state.

Westbury Court is one of very few formal water gardens of the late seventeenth century to have survived in England. It was clearly modelled on Dutch gardens of the period, combining formal canals and pavilions with carefully planned, small-scale planting. Due in part to neglect, the garden had remained largely unchanged into the twentieth century, but by the early 1960s it was in a perilous state. It had come into the ownership of a property developer who wanted to demolish the wonderful gazebo at one end of the main canal and build houses on the site. The local council fortunately refused planning permission and approached the National Trust. Although the trust had never before taken on a such a derelict property, it was able to commit to restoration with the help of a grant from the Historic Buildings Council, combined with money raised in a public appeal and a particularly generous donation.

Work began in 1967. The practical limits imposed are described by John Sales, who for many years was intimately involved in the management of the Trust's gardens: "The layout had to be adapted radically for upkeep by one gardener and the restoration involved compromises." While Sales concedes that a careful archaeological investigation would precede any reconstruction work today, he comments: "All restored gardens

are the products of the values and understanding of those who restore them as well as being a reflection of the past … Westbury needs to be seen in the light of the date of its restoration, taking into account the resources and expertise then available." (Sales, 2001: 31).

As with many similar projects undertaken in subsequent years, contemporary evidence (even if limited) would be the key to historical accuracy. In the case of Westbury Court, a vital source of information lay in the detailed bird's-eye view engraved by Johannes Kip in 1707, while in the county record office were found the account books belonging to the garden's creator, Maynard Colchester. Restoration required the two canals to be dredged and the main gazebo to be reconstructed. For the parterre beside the canals, and also in the small flower garden with its own brick pavilion, plants were chosen from those mentioned in Colchester's account books, or were varieties known to have been grown at the time. This garden could so easily have disappeared completely, but its change of fortunes has provided us with a restored gem of great rarity.

OPPOSITE
The little brick gazebo at Westbury Court, Gloucestershire, has its own secret flower garden. It was replanted with period accuracy when, in the 1960s, the National Trust decided to undertake its first major garden restoration.

ABOVE
A parterre lies to one side of the canals at Westbury Court, which was modelled on Dutch gardens and is one of England's few formal water gardens surviving from the late seventeenth century.

Château de Vaux-le-Vicomte

In contrast to Westbury Court, a little-known garden preserved as a rare example of a vanished style, the Château de Vaux-le-Vicomte in France is surrounded by one of the world's most famous gardens. It was this pre-eminent status that motivated Alfred Sommier to begin restoration in the nineteenth century, having acquired the estate in 1875. Regardless of the royal claims of Versailles, for many people Vaux-le-Vicomte is France's supreme formal garden. As the first of the great classical palaces, it marks the start of the century-long period during which French design came to dominate Europe.

The garden was created in 1656–61 for Louis XIV's finance minister, Nicolas Fouquet, by the triumvirate who would later work for the king at Versailles: André Le Nôtre as garden designer, Louis Le Vau as architect, and Charles Le Brun as artist. The lavish design incorporated parterres with further areas of formal gardens leading out to woodland walks on the adjacent hillside. *Bassins* (formal pools) were positioned to create reflections, while fountains, canals, and cascades were concealed on cross-axes.

At the point when Alfred Sommier acquired Vaux-le-Vicomte, the garden had been left uncultivated for two decades and, not surprisingly, its fundamental quality was compromised. The symmetry between the moated palace and its surroundings had become unbalanced. It was the return of a sense of control, as well as the replacement of missing key features, that Alfred Sommier aimed to achieve by restoration. During the following 15 years, and with the participation of designer Gabriel Hippolyte Destailleurs, garden buildings were restored, missing statues replaced, and hedges and topiary pruned back to their correct proportions. After Sommier's death in 1893, his son completed the work to the garden. In particular, he commissioned the leading French revivalist garden designer of the time, Achille Duchêne, to reinstate the parterres immediately around the palace.

Alteration or restoration?

In the past, the chief criticisms levelled at garden restoration arose mainly from projects carried out before the beginning of the twentieth century, which were seen as alterations rather than genuine restorations. While the work might have refreshed

LEFT
Château de Vaux-le-Vicomte was created in 1656–61 for Louis XIV's finance minister, Nicolas Fouquet. Today, it stands as an outstanding example of the early twentieth-century restorations carried out to revive the glory of French formal gardens.

OPPOSITE
The intricate parterres beside the palace at Vaux-le-Vicomte were reconstructed with reference to contemporary engravings. Pools, statuary, and a tree-lined vista complete the picture.

a garden's appearance, critics argued that it detracted from the original integrity of the place. A number of the most famous gardens in Germany were subjected to a series of such alterations in the late eighteenth to nineteenth centuries, which kept them in a rejuvenated state but at the same time tended to result in a confusing miscellany.

The late eighteenth century was in any case a time of change in German gardens, where the English Landscape style had become fashionable. Parks were being laid out around existing formal gardens, or the two merged together. One such was the garden at Augustusburg, originally designed in grand baroque style for the Archbishop of Cologne in the early eighteenth century. In the 1840s, however, the emphasis of the garden was changed by the leading designer of the time, Peter Joseph Lenné, who added a picturesque park in the surrounding area. In the 1930s, extensive alterations were again made to the parterre under the guise of restoration, which further confused the picture.

Both garden and palace were destroyed during World War II, leading to another restoration in 1947. This time it was decided to return as closely as possible to the original eighteenth-century design, with an intricate pattern of *broderie* in the parterre, and enclosing avenues of newly planted pleached lime trees. Of the ornaments damaged in the war, none of those added to the parterre after its initial design were replaced. The current garden may be a reconstruction, but it was nonetheless reconstructed with careful attention to historical accuracy.

Painswick House

The restoration of a large-scale formal garden such as Augustusburg will always require an element of reconstruction, although the underlying geometrical symmetry of the design can often be reinstated with precision. Replacement plants, hedges, and trees can be put back in their original positions within the surviving framework of paths, steps, pools, and

OPPOSITE
The classical
eighteenth-century
palace and baroque
garden at Augustusburg,
commissioned by the
Archbishop of Cologne
but not completed until
after his death, were
extensively damaged
during World War II. The
palace had to be rebuilt.

BELOW
In a display of formal
grandeur, the French-
inspired *parterre de
broderie* at Augustusburg
swirls around circular
pools and is enclosed
by pleached lime trees.
The parterre was
reconstructed in the
1840s, the 1930s, and
again in 1947.

fountains. A more natural style of garden, such as the rococo landscape at Painswick House, in Gloucestershire, requires a different approach. The framework of this type of design is far looser, depending for effect on the growth of trees and the siting of temples or pavilions.

Often the largest threat to these landscapes is posed by their size: many of the parks laid out by Lancelot "Capability" Brown, the best-known English garden designer of the eighteenth century, have partially or wholly disappeared in recent times because they were close to motorways or towns in need of expansion. Restoration is often impossible in such cases, but where it is feasible, the vital work needed is to repair or rebuild damaged buildings, to replace paths, and to replant trees according to the original layout.

The challenges of this particular sort of landscape restoration are well illustrated by Painswick. Hanging in the

OPPOSITE TOP AND BOTTOM
All trace of the delightful rococo garden at Painswick House, Gloucestershire, had long disappeared by the time sensitive restoration began to bring it back to life. Its pavilions and wooded setting were designed to evoke a Gothic atmosphere.

ABOVE
Historical research in the 1980s suggested that a watercolour of *c.*1748, which hung at Painswick House, did in fact depict the garden accurately. When this was confirmed by archaeology, the painting became the blueprint for restoration.

LEFT
A carpet of snowdrops naturalized under beech trees is the only flowering feature in the landscape, and recalls the galanthophile James Atkins, who lived at Painswick in the nineteenth century.

house is a painting by Thomas Robins, dated 1748. It shows a woodland garden theatrically ornamented with pavilions in a manner that exemplifies the rococo style which fleetingly touched English gardens in the early eighteenth century. By the late twentieth century, all evidence of such a garden had disappeared, and the scene had become a beautiful but unadorned wooded valley.

It was not known whether Robins' painting depicted a true scene or was pure fantasy until an initial investigation in the mid-1980s by two garden and architectural historians, Timothy Mowl and Roger White, suggested that it might indeed be an accurate record of the original garden. The owner of Painswick, Lord Dickinson, bravely decided to reinstate the design. As work progressed, archaeology confirmed many details shown in the painting, such as the siting of paths and the position of buildings, and these confirmed the location of vistas through trees.

Almost the greatest challenge at Painswick has been the fund-raising needed to finance the restoration of the extraordinary Gothic temples. With work now complete, this inherently natural scene is once again embellished in rococo style. And the description of Painswick recorded by Bishop Pococke after a visit in 1757 still holds true: "A very pretty garden ... cut into walks through wood and adorn'd with water and buildings." (Taylor, 2003: 220).

HET LOO AND HAMPTON COURT PALACE

Even though Painswick was restored with the light touch required by that particular style of garden, it was solid archaeological evidence that proved conclusive in establishing the identity of the original. In recent decades, archaeology has become increasingly important in the field of restoration. It played a particularly significant role in the twin restorations of two of Europe's most prestigious royal gardens, Het Loo in the Netherlands and Hampton Court Palace in England, both originally designed in the seventeenth century for William of Orange. Restoration at Het Loo began in the 1970s, followed by Hampton Court in the 1990s. In both cases, the clear intention was to ensure the highest-possible level of historical accuracy by unearthing archaeological evidence.

The garden at Het Loo was laid out to complement the new palace built by William in place of the old hunting lodge he had purchased in 1684. It was to prove the most ambitious baroque garden in the Dutch style ever created. The series of great parterres was designed by Dutch architect Jacob Roman, with contributions from other designers and the French Huguenot artist-gardener, Daniel Marot. Most impressive of all is the Great Garden, which is divided into two areas. The lower section, with eight parterres decorated by fountains, is located

OPPOSITE
Long, arched bowers draped with climbing plants are a feature of the late seventeenth-century garden at Het Loo, which was restored to its baroque splendour when the palace became a national museum in the 1970s.

LEFT
The original patterns for Het Loo's eight parterres were identified by archaeology. Exhaustive research of this sort made it one of the most historically accurate large-scale garden restorations of the twentieth century.

ABOVE
Het Loo was the palace built in the Netherlands for Prince William of Orange. Its formal garden was largely replaced by a landscape park in the nineteenth century, but survived in contemporary descriptions and plans.

immediately in front of the palace, while the upper area beyond has a large octagonal basin as its centrepiece. In William's era, the intricate patterns of clipped hedges and topiary were matched by the superlative quality of the garden ornaments.

After the death of William in 1702, the gardens at Het Loo survived throughout most of the eighteenth century. Yet changes crept in from 1795, when the Netherlands fell to France and the palace was abandoned by the royal family. In 1806, Napoleon made his brother, Louis Bonaparte, king of Holland, and Het Loo was selected as a residence by the new monarch. He set about altering the palace, and in 1808 replaced some of the garden with a landscape park. Further changes followed after the return of the Dutch royal family, who extended the park, created two large lakes, and added exotic trees and an arboretum. By the end of the nineteenth century, the parterres and avenues of the original formal garden had largely disappeared.

The possibility of restoration was first considered during the 1950s, but was not acted upon until 1978. By that time, Het Loo had become state property following the death of Queen Wilhelmina. The palace was to open as a national museum honouring the royal family, having been restored to its original seventeenth-century appearance by the removal of later additions; the garden's grand formality was also to be reinstated. Supervised by garden architect J B Baron van Asbeck, the work was based on archaeological research, by which the lines and foundations of the original layout were revealed; and on contemporary records, including a detailed description of the gardens recorded by William's private physician, Dr Walter Harris, and published in London in 1699 as *A description of the King's Royal Palace and Gardens at Loo*. In addition, use was made of a garden plan, dated *c*.1714, made by Christiaan Pieter van Staden.

Van Asbeck's approach to the restoration was exhaustive. A series of working parties was formed to agree the exact basis of each element of the project. Whether in replanting the parterres or rebuilding the fountains, historical accuracy was paramount. It is not surprising that van Asbeck wrote afterwards, with some satisfaction, "No other historical garden has gained such international celebrity immediately after its construction, vanished from the face of the earth after 115 years and, finally, 175 years later, been restored in all its former

RIGHT
With statues and swan figures regilded, this fountain at Het Loo looks as good as new. Water is a recurring motif, as is the conical topiary seen behind.

glory as though time had stood still for the intervening three centuries." (Plumptre, 2005: 144).

While the restoration at Het Loo encompassed virtually all of the original garden, the parallel project carried out later at Hampton Court Palace focused on the Privy Garden. This was the garden created for William and his English wife, Mary, who ruled as joint monarchs of England from 1689. It lay between the new part of the palace, built for them by Sir Christopher Wren, and the river Thames, and had originally been a long, rectangular parterre similar in design to parts of Het Loo. Daniel Marot, William's gardener in the Netherlands, was probably involved in the design. Overlooked on both sides by raised walks, the garden's main axis led to a spectacular focal point along the riverside boundary: a screen of gilded wrought-iron panels made by the royal craftsman Jean Tijou.

The parterre was allowed to grow into maturity through the eighteenth century, but during the nineteenth century its detailed outlines began to disappear under Victorian shrubberies and the uncontrolled growth of yew trees. By the time the decision to restore had been taken, all views from the palace to the river had also been obscured. Most of the statuary had been removed, and Tijou's glittering screen had long been painted black.

Inspired by the pioneering example of Het Loo, a thorough archaeological survey of the Privy Garden was carried out to reveal, with great accuracy, the outlines of the original design. These were reinstated, then replanting began. Young yew trees

ABOVE
The Privy Garden dates from the reign of William of Orange, king of England from 1689–1702. Changes made during the Victorian era led to its disappearance beneath the unchecked growth of trees and shrubs.

OPPOSITE
The manner in which
the rectangular parterre
of the Privy Garden was
designed to fill the space
between the palace and
the river Thames is
shown by this aerial
view, taken after the
1990s restoration.

BELOW
One of the most
adventurous details
of Hampton Court's
restoration was the re-
gilding of Jean Tijou's
masterly wrought-iron
screen for the garden's
riverside boundary,
which had been painted
black for centuries.

and hollies were propagated from what was identified as the original stock of topiary. Other plants for the parterres were chosen from contemporary lists, including two plant orders dating from 1701. The original air of royal splendour was restored with the regilding of Tijou's screen and the copies made from surviving statues. In the immediate aftermath of the work, as happens with many such restorations, the most striking feature was the almost unnatural newness of the garden and the sensation that it had greatly increased in size. The Privy Garden, a rare surviving example of seventeenth-century formality, had regained its intended scale.

LA MAJORELLE

Nothing could be more different to the grand symmetry of Het Loo and Hampton Court than the painterly exoticism of La Majorelle in Morocco, which reflects the flamboyant style of both its creator and restorer. The garden was made in the 1920s by French artist Jacques Majorelle (whose father, Louis, was famous as the designer of art nouveau furniture) and was purchased in the 1980s by legendary fashion designer, Yves Saint Laurent. Aside from the inherent interest of its design and

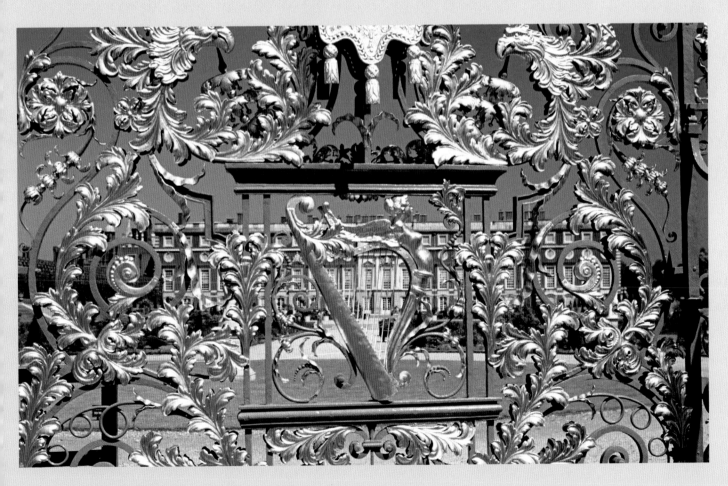

the sensitivity of the restoration, the garden's close association with the personalities of Majorelle and Saint Laurent marks it out as unusual.

Known for its intense colours, particularly the cobalt blue paint used to link canals, fountains and other architectural features throughout the garden, La Majorelle was an extension of Louis Majorelle's avant-garde paintings. The bold originality of the design, with its dense, highly sculptural planting, was what appealed to Yves Saint Laurent when he took up the challenge of reversing the decline. With the faded palette of blue, yellow, pink, and green paint now revived, the garden reflects Majorelle's original concept: the brilliant colours look right in strong sunlight. And nearly a century after it was created, La Majorelle still leaves a vivid impression as one of the most innovative gardens of its time. Elements of the restoration also demonstrate how subtle changes can bring a garden up to date and yet retain the vital connection with its creator. The studio Jacques Majorelle sited in the middle of his garden has been retained, but now houses a small museum of Islamic art.

SHALIMAR BAGH

Many garden restorations are carried out as a result of personal passion, but equally influential in current times is the growing reach of conservation bodies. A number of gardens discussed in this book were restored only after being placed on UNESCO's list of World Heritage Sites, which generally targets historically important landscapes that are considered to be under threat. Although in many cases the restoration work is not comprehensive, it is important that these gardens are at least saved from destruction and can benefit from greater security.

A good example is Shalimar Bagh, located 5.5km (3.5 miles) from the city of Lahore, in Pakistan. This outstanding Mughal garden has been one of the country's six World Heritage Sites since 1991. However, a crisis occurred in 1999 when a road was widened on the garden's southern boundary, with the result that vital water tanks, built more than 300 years ago to supply the garden's fountains, were destroyed. The Pakistan government communicated its concerns about Shalimar Bagh to

OPPOSITE
The unusual restoration
at La Majorelle,
Morocco, was initiated
in the 1980s by
legendary couturier
Yves Saint Laurent.
His desire to rescue the
faded property adds to
the fascination of this
painterly garden.

ABOVE
Every detail of the
bold design, from the
sculptural planting to
the cobalt blue
woodwork, emphasizes
the bold style of Jacques
Majorelle, the French
artist who created the
garden in the 1920s.

UNESCO, and the garden was quickly placed on the much
more select list of "Sites in Danger".

Shalimar Bagh is a celebration of water, created in the 1640s
to mark the completion of a canal bringing water to Lahore
from the river Ravi. The garden was built at the behest of Shah
Jahan, the fifth Mughal Emperor, whose most famous landmark
is the Taj Mahal at Agra. Shalimar Bagh is a remarkable and
grandiose example of the *chahar bagh*, the classic design for
Mughal gardens, in which a square is divided into four sections
by canals. At Shalimar Bagh there are two *chahar bagh* patterns
separated by a central rectangular terrace where a massive
reservoir of water measuring more than 60m (200ft) across was
originally enlivened by 250 fountains. The design as a whole
forms three gently descending terraces. White marble was used
for the main architectural ornaments, such as the emperor's
throne and various pavilions, while patterned bricks were used
for the enclosing walls and alcoves.

Much of the original splendour and beauty of the garden
diminished some time ago; the sumptuous decorations made

from marble and agate have been replaced with inferior materials. Nonetheless, the garden still presents an informative picture of a rare survival. Without the intervention of UNESCO, Shalimar Bagh might not have escaped destruction. It is now in a position to benefit from further restoration in the future.

HELIGAN

If there is a single project that catapulted garden restoration out of the restricted worlds of garden history and archaeology and into the public consciousness, it has to be the 1990s restoration of the English "Lost Gardens of Heligan", masterminded by former pop impresario Tim Smit. Of course, this was not the first instance of a restoration project to help its cause by driving its own publicity, but it has certainly been one of the most successful. The initial story has almost assumed the aura of folklore: Smit, on a chance visit, was shown the derelict and overgrown site of the former garden by a surviving member of the family that had owned Heligan for centuries. Fired with enthusiasm, but by his own admission hopelessly ignorant of horticulture, Smit proceeded to apply his formidable marketing powers to raising sufficient funds – all from private sources – for the restoration. He then oversaw the work that was carried out over a five-year period with the help of a team of volunteers.

BELOW
The great Mughal garden of Shalimar Bagh in Pakistan, with its canals, paved walks, and distinctive pavilions laid out on three gently descending terraces, was completed in 1640 for Emperor Shah Jahan.

LEFT
The garden's restoration followed its listing as a UNESCO World Heritage Site in 1981. Even so, plans to widen an adjacent road in 1999 posed a threat to the garden's magnificent water features.

RIGHT
Heligan is remarkable for the way that its restoration captured the public imagination in England. Crowds came to see the Cornish garden that had slumbered for decades and been brought back to life in the 1990s.

BELOW
The Tremayne family gardened at Heligan from the sixteenth century, landscaped the grounds, and made use of the sheltered, coastal site for a collection of exotic plants assembled in the nineteenth century.

OPPOSITE
One of the attractive features of the restoration at Heligan is the way it illustrates historic gardening techniques, including the skill that went into running a kitchen garden and growing pineapples under glass.

Following a best-selling book and a television series, Heligan became the most-visited garden in Cornwall: quite an achievement in a county that boasts some of the United Kingdom's favourite gardens. The whole project had caught the public imagination. Smit played on the idea that this old family garden, cherished in the eighteenth and nineteenth centuries by a number of rather outstanding horticulturists, had gone to sleep early in the twentieth century and entered a downward spiral after World War II. It is a scenario that the supporters of subsequent restoration projects have adapted with enthusiasm – at Serre de la Madone in France, for instance, as well as at Aberglasney in Wales (see pages 46 and 56).

Smit managed to popularize the gardening techniques of the eighteenth and early nineteenth centuries. He enthralled a non-specialist audience, even reaching people who had no particular interest in horticulture, with tales of skills that have long disappeared from English gardens. Melons and pineapples were once grown in the walled garden at Heligan, and the special hothouses and pits constructed for this purpose were rebuilt during restoration. Smit suggested that many principles of today's organic gardening can be traced back to earlier practices, pointing out how recesses in the garden's walls show that bees were kept at Heligan as an aid to pollination. Outside the walled garden, the collection of exotic trees planted in the nineteenth century was linked to the heroics of Victorian plant hunters.

While Heligan is certainly an historical curiosity, it would never have rated among the cognoscenti as an outstanding garden. Yet this case nicely illustrates how a garden's rank as an aesthetic or technical creation does not necessarily determine the value of its restoration. The publicity Smit generated for Heligan has, as the garden writer Patrick Taylor observes, "done the cause of garden conservation a great deal of good" (Taylor, 2003: 42). A more tangible consequence of Smit's success at Heligan is that it led him on to the Eden Project, arguably the most ambitious horticultural project seen worldwide in modern times.

KAUFMANN "DESERT HOUSE"

Heligan was in many ways a very modern restoration project, using publicity, the media, and public interest to further its aims. But in looking back to a period of garden-making that was so strikingly different to our own, it was by its nature retrospective. During the 1990s, when Heligan was being restored, a contrasting project with its own distinct set of ambitions and principles was under way at the Kaufmann "Desert House" in California.

Looking at photographs of the ultra-modern Kaufmann house and its surrounding desert garden, it is hard to imagine that any restoration could have been necessary. But the advent of modernist houses and gardens (almost invariably designed as a single entity) brought a new dimension to garden restoration: short-term work is needed to maintain the close detail on which the often minimalist whole depends for effect. The Kaufmann house was sold in the 1990s, and the new owners decided to return it to the original concept. They were aware that various post-design alterations had changed the appearance and character of both house and garden.

They could hardly have chosen a more iconic piece of architecture, designed in 1946 by the Austrian-born Richard

Neutra. He is widely regarded as California's outstanding modernist architect of the 1940s and 1950s, at a time when the West Coast state was blazing a trail in modernist architecture and garden design. His client was the department store owner Edgar J Kaufmann, who had earlier commissioned a modernist design for Fallingwater, his Pennsylvania home, which was designed by Frank Lloyd Wright. The "Desert House" was his summer retreat, and its design harnessed the impact of the spectacular desert setting. The house is constructed in a series of horizontal planes, and the planting scheme for the garden celebrates the native plants of the surrounding landscape.

The restoration was carried out in consultation with the architectural partnership of Marmol Radziner and was based on a series of famous black-and-white photographs of the property that were taken in 1947 by Julius Shulman. The most urgent work in the garden (which had greatly expanded in size since first laid out) was to remove an accumulation of non-native plants that diluted the sense of the desert landscape coming right up to the house and crowded out views: both crucial elements of Neutra's plan. The restoration was completed in 1998.

ABOVE
Tall picture windows
ensure that the low-level
house merges seamlessly
into the surrounding
garden, thus fulfilling
what is a crucial
principle of modernist
garden design.

RIGHT
A modernist landscape demands close attention to detail for it to remain true to the original concept. At the Kaufmann "Desert House", the addition of non-native plants had diluted the impact of the garden and were removed.

GARLAND FARM – AND BEYOND

As final proof of the variety of incentives that lie behind garden restoration, we come to Garland Farm, the last home of Beatrix Farrand, one of America's most revered landscape designers. She lived for many years at Reef Point, Bar Harbor, Maine, on the American East Coast, and intended to bequeath her enormous plant collection to a school of horticulture. None had been found by the time she was 83, so she took her favourite plants, her picket fencing and ornaments, and moved to nearby Garland Farm.

Few people knew that Garland Farm existed, but in 2002 landscape architect Patrick Chasse discovered the small garden Farrand created here in the last three years of her life; a chance event such as this often determines whether an important garden survives or disappears. Chasse founded the Beatrix Farrand Society, which raised the funds needed to purchase Garland Farm. Now that the site is listed by the National Register of Historic Places, restoration is continuing with reference to an historical and horticultural report produced by

a firm of architects. Detailed analysis and planning have become an essential part of today's assiduous garden restoration.

The themes explored and developed in this book confirm that there is no single type of garden restoration; the subject is increasingly diverse. In general terms, however, restoration is prompted when neglect, organic evolution or third-party intervention threaten a garden felt to represent a particular style or the work of an admired individual. But there are other factors uniting the different restorations described in these pages: the quest for authenticity, the requirement for high standards of work, and the commitment to rebuilding something of sufficient value to merit the effort and expense. There is no doubt that a garden's original genius can be revitalized by restoration.

Aside from the inevitable demises resulting from the passage of time, scores of historically important gardens have been lost to neglect. In today's conservation-conscious world, this is surely a cause for regret. The appetite and resources for restoration will grow and, in all probability, the expertise with which they are carried out will do likewise.

LEFT
Reflecting the brilliant sunshine, the swimming pool at the "Desert House" reinforces the contrast between the clean-cut, horizontal lines of Neutra's modern architecture and the wild landscape beyond.

THE ART OF RESTORATION

Garden restoration is, by definition, a practical operation. It requires a clear plan: one that usually includes removing decay, reversing neglect, and taming plant growth that has run wild to the detriment of the overall picture. But as all successful restoration projects demonstrate (and not least the three very different gardens that are featured in this chapter), there is also an intangible element to the process. This can be called the art of restoration for the way it achieves harmony between evidence or inspiration from the past and aspirations for the garden's future.

Château de Villandry

TOURS • FRANCE

The great majority of gardens discussed in gardening literature have been restored relatively recently – certainly since World War II. By contrast, the restoration at the Château de Villandry, located just west of Tours in France, dates from the early years of the twentieth century. For decades after it was complete, at a time when restoration was not always approved of by garden historians and designers, it was widely accepted as an inspired example of the art of restoration carried out to the highest standard. Indeed, it has been the model cited to justify many other restorations and has become one of the best-known and most popular gardens in the world.

The Renaissance château stands on a broad, flat site beside the river Cher, a short distance upstream from where it flows into the larger river Loire. The château was built during the 1530s by Jean Le Breton, finance minister to King François I, who was the most important builder and gardener among French kings prior to Louis XIV. When Le Breton replaced the original twelfth-century castle, he retained only the battlemented tower, and this survives today as a visual contrast to the elegant facade of his later building. He surrounded his

BELOW
A ramped retaining wall and rows of pleached limes on the terrace behind the Garden of Music indicate the larger structure of the garden surrounding this detailed parterre.

OPPOSITE
The close relationship between the patterns of planting and the stone facade of the Renaissance château have always been fundamental to the appeal of Villandry.

OPPOSITE
The *potager's* summer tapestry of geometric shapes and varied textures is formed by box-edged blocks of vegetables, which are punctuated at intervals with brightly planted urns.

ABOVE
Looking from the world-famous *potager*, or kitchen garden, back towards the château, the raised level of the upper terrace in the background contrasts with the horizontal lines of the planting.

RIGHT
An early twentieth-century view of Villandry reveals the immaculate lines of the garden as they were when freshly restored by Joachim Carvallo, owner of the estate from 1906.

château with extensive formal Renaissance gardens, but alterations to these began during the eighteenth century, when Château de Villandry was acquired by the Marquis de Castellane. Le Breton's garden had disappeared by the early nineteenth century, having been replaced by a *jardin à l'anglaise* as was fashionable at the time.

The château subsequently underwent several changes in ownership and suffered a number of unhappy architectural additions during the nineteenth century. Then in 1906 it was acquired by Dr Joachim Carvallo, who was originally from Spain, and his American wife, Ann Coleman; the couple had met in Paris, where both were studying medicine. Villandry and its restoration were to become their lifelong passion, and the meticulous standards set by the Carvallos are maintained with equal energy today by their grandson.

Carvallo did not have detailed evidence of the Renaissance gardens that surrounded Le Breton's sixteenth-century château, but he determined to restore the building as authentically as possible by removing the later additions and to style the gardens in such a way that would evoke the spirit and appearance of the Renaissance original. Work began in 1907 and continued until 1920. The garden's moats had been filled in during the eighteenth century to create terraces and canals, which in turn disappeared under the *jardin à l'anglaise*. Once these pre-nineteenth century features were uncovered and restored, the gardens had a framework of formal terraced space and water within which Carvallo could work.

He made up for the lack of historical evidence about the garden's early design by studying the most significant record of French sixteenth-century gardens, written by the architect and artist Jacques Androuet du Cerceau. Entitled *Les Plus Excellents Bastiments de France*, and published in two volumes in 1576 and 1579, the work contains engravings and descriptions of the great gardens of the time. Carvallo also familiarized himself with another sixteenth-century book, *Monasticum Gallicanum*, written by Benedictine monks. In keeping with the period of Le Breton's château, Carvallo wanted a garden that belonged to the humanist early-Renaissance period and looked back in time to the decorative, productive gardens of monasteries, rather than forward to the grandeur of the French classical gardens of the seventeenth century.

Carvallo recreated a series of different gardens on the three tiers of terraces that run along two adjacent sides of the château. On the same level as the ground-floor windows of the building are the ornamental flower gardens, where a canal divides two adjoining rectangular areas of formal beds that are punctuated with yew topiary and fountains. In keeping with the character of Renaissance gardens, they are allegorical in tone. The Garden of Love, for example, formed of four box-edged squares, with patterns of clipped box and annual flowers, symbolizes the four forms of profane love: adulterous, tragic, passionate, and tender. In the second area is the Garden of Music, where another pattern of box-edged beds contains a mixture of low shrubs and herbaceous plants, some planted in shapes to suggest musical instruments.

On the level above the ornamental gardens is a large formal pool, surrounded by lawn and a pattern of smaller pools, providing a contrast of cool serenity. This upper terrace is partially enclosed by raised walkways shaded by pleached lime trees, where visitors can look down onto Villandry's most famous feature, the formal kitchen garden or *potager*, laid out on the lowest terrace. Here, a symmetrical series of nine box-edged squares, each divided into a different pattern of beds, are planted with spring and summer displays of fruit and vegetables. Ornamental annuals and biennials are used to decorate the narrow beds that run around the perimeter of each square, and rose-covered arbours stand at the corners. The planting displays, which are not intended as an illustration of plants that would have been available in the sixteenth century, are never the same from one year to the next, combining brilliant colours and varied foliage within an overall orderliness. The effect is something no visitor forgets.

The scale of the gardens is prodigious – and not just because they cover 7ha (17 acres). Large quantities of plants are required for the programme of bedding schemes (an estimated 30,000 are raised annually from seed to create the patterns); and then there is the labour of clipping some 32km (20 miles) of box hedges, as well as topiary yew trees to trim and lime trees to pleach. It is all still done by hand. Indeed, the whole garden is run on strictly traditional lines, with no electrical machinery or weedkillers.

It is clear that Château de Villandry was never intended to be an historically precise reconstruction in the way that has been attempted at other gardens, where detailed research into their past appearance has been aided by a greater quantity of surviving evidence. The memorable quality of Villandry, however, is that it continues to embody Joachim Carvallo's determination to recreate not just a château and its garden, but the Renaissance philosophy and way of life that they represent. Equally significant is the fact that Villandry continues to be acknowledged as a pre-eminent garden restoration and a shining example to anyone who is about to embark on a similar project.

OPPOSITE
The use of massed
groups of a single kind
of plant, their bright
hues balanced by the
repeating dark green of
clipped yew, is central
to the garden's impact.

LEFT
This corner of the
potager illustrates how
the garden's architectural
structure provides a
highly decorative
framework for the
annual cycle of
planting schemes.

Serre de la Madone

Lawrence Johnston showed extraordinary skill as a designer and plantsman in the way he developed his garden at Serre de la Madone in the South of France. He spent more than 30 years creating the brilliant ensemble of a classical design incorporating dramatic elements, combined with planting that was carefully organized and often exotic. It was always a private garden in Johnston's lifetime, but its reputation spread by word of mouth – at first among the gardening friends that Johnston entertained there, and then to a widening audience of cognoscenti fortunate enough to visit.

After Johnston's death in 1958, the property remained in private ownership for four decades, and the garden gradually lost its special quality. By the end of the century, it was on the verge of vanishing for good. In 1999, Serre de la Madone was acquired by the Conservatoire du Littoral (the French government agency that protects endangered natural shoreline and lakeside sites). The garden is being restored in a sensitive, artistic way, with the aim that it should once again evoke Johnston's achievements.

Few amateur gardeners create a garden that becomes internationally famous; Johnston belongs to the select band celebrated for two such gardens. Born in Paris in 1871, he was brought up in France by his wealthy American mother, Gertrude Winthrop. He attended Trinity College, Cambridge, then in 1900 adopted British citizenship, joined the army, and fought first in the war against the Afrikaners in South Africa and then in World War I, attaining the rank of major. After his return, he settled at Hidcote Bartram Manor, the Gloucestershire farm his mother had purchased for him in 1907. It was here that he began creating what would become one of England's most influential twentieth-century gardens.

Johnston's gardening appetite and abilities grew with experience, and by the 1920s, when the increasingly admired garden at Hidcote had matured, he was seeking a fresh challenge. The French Riviera attracted him both for its plant-growing opportunities and as a mild winter retreat; it was also where his mother lived during the latter years of her life. In

OPPOSITE
Serre de la Madone's central vista illustrates how brilliantly its design balances the vertical movement towards the villa against the cross-axes of the ascending terraces.

RIGHT
Lawrence Johnston chose this specific spot in the water terrace as the perfect position for his statue of Venus.

1924, Johnston purchased a plot of land with a modest farmhouse in the Gorbio Valley, to the west of Menton. Over the next few years, he would add to the property with judicious purchases of neighbouring parcels of land, until Serre de la Madone covered 6ha (15 acres) and reached the top of the hill where unbroken views extended to the Mediterranean.

The Riviera of the 1920s had its own tradition of gardening, both among French inhabitants and expatriates from England and America. Johnston's distinguished gardening neighbours included Vicomte Charles de Noailles, a renowned plantsman who in 1928 commissioned a remarkable modernist garden for his villa at Hyères; Edith Wharton, the American novelist and garden historian; and Ernest de Ganay, one of France's leading garden designers and writers. What made Johnston unusual, perhaps, was that he did the gardening himself – not alone, however, because a head gardener and staff of 11 ensured that the garden developed rapidly and was immaculately maintained. Ernest de Ganay recalled a visit to Serre de la Madone when Johnston came out to greet him wearing velvet corduroy trousers, his hands stained with earth (Russell, 1993: 97).

The sheltered, densely wooded hillside at Serre de la Madone guaranteed a wonderful, frost-free mildness and, along with generous rainfall and summer warmth, offered luxuriant growing conditions. Here Johnston indulged his love of plants in a spectacular fashion. He skilfully grew exotics and rarities from

ABOVE
An ornamental stone doorway typifies both the elements of surprise and the architectural decoration that Johnston incorporated into the garden.

RIGHT
This photograph was taken shortly after Johnston's death in 1958. With a baroque flourish, the lower section of the central staircase divides theatrically into two curving flights of steps.

around the world that would never have survived the bitter, windy Cotswold winter at Hidcote, making use of the ancient, irregular terraces originally used for cultivating grapes and olives.

The combination of climate and terrain gave Johnston an opportunity to garden with bravado, and he embraced it with enthusiasm. The farmhouse towards the top of the site was expanded into the present elegant villa, and the series of terraces were enhanced with pools, fountains, statuary, and a rotunda-style belvedere commanding a fine view. Of the three pools on the broadest terrace, one was kept clear of plants to provide the maximum surface of water for reflection, while the others were planted with lotus and water lilies.

This architectural setting was embellished by Johnston's dramatic use of planting. The range of plants he grew at Serre de la Madone was extraordinary: towering ornamental trees such as the *Magnolia delavayi* that still survives from Johnston's time; climbers such as the wisteria and evergreen clematis with which he clothed the long pergola; an array of rare shrubs that included *Buddleja officinalis*, which bears clusters of mauve flowers in winter, and collections of camellias and bottlebrushes (*Callistemon* species); as well as night-flowering exotics such as the cactus *Cereus* (now classified as *Selenicereus*). Smaller plants were often massed in blocks of a single kind to produce flamboyant displays, using iris, scarlet-and-white striped Lady tulips (*Tulipa clusiana*), bright-pink belladonna lilies (*Amaryllis belladonna*), and selections of South African bulbs. And yet the quantity of plants never submerged the meticulous planning of the garden. Each terrace and area retained its own identity.

ABOVE
Rows of clipped hedges are a continuation of the horizontal lines formed by the main terraces and also offset the varied colours of the flowering plants.

Of all his gardening exploits, it was as a plant collector that Johnston wished to be remembered. In 1927, he travelled to South Africa with Collingwood "Cherry" Ingram and Sir George Ingram, both horticulturists and plant collectors, and sent back quantities of plants to Serre de la Madone, including rare tulips and other bulbs, pelargoniums, and plumbago. The following year he went to East Africa, and then in 1931 he accompanied the great Scottish plant collector George Forrest on his last expedition to Yunnan in China. Forrest was spartan in character and did not take to Johnston as a "gentleman-gardener", but that did not interfere with Johnston's plant collecting. Among the tender, evergreen treasures that he discovered and sent back to thrive at Serre de la Madone were *Jasminum polyanthum*, a climber with fragrant white flowers, and

BELOW
The sheltered site and mild climate at Serre de la Madone allowed Johnston to pursue his interest in exotic, sculptural plants. Restoration has involved replanting some of the key species.

one of the garden's most magnificent shrubs, yellow-flowered *Mahonia siamensis*. Other trips were made to Mexico (the fruits of which were planted in an eponymous area of the garden), Japan, and the French Alps.

In 1948, Johnston left England to live permanently at Serre de la Madone for the good of his health (he was suffering from the onset of Alzheimer's disease). Hidcote was offered to the National Trust and became the first property it took on primarily for the importance of its garden. Although Hidcote has changed in the ensuing decades, it is still one of the trust's most highly prized and widely visited properties.

It is fascinating to compare the gardens at Hidcote and Serre de la Madone for their similarities and differences during Johnston's lifetime and, more particularly, for their fortunes after

his death. Hidcote is a classic masterpiece combining garden design and plantsmanship in a way that is elegantly understated and unquestionably English. Serre de la Madone's richer character was described by Ernest de Ganay as "an oasis of flowers, a paradise of colours and scents, sheltered by wild surrounding hills" (Jones, 2003: 26). While Hidcote became a national institution, its counterpart slid towards decline.

Johnston bequeathed Serre de la Madone to Nancy Lindsay, the daughter of his lifelong friend, Norah Lindsay, who was a garden designer and the creator of an acclaimed garden at Sutton Courtenay in Oxfordshire. Nancy Lindsay followed the family tradition in being a keen gardener, but she never had the resources to maintain the property and eventually had to sell it. Much of the garden's statuary was sold or given away, along with other ornaments and many plants. The two subsequent owners, Sir Evelyn Baring, who was the retired governor of Kenya, and Comte Jacques de Würstemberger, a wealthy Belgian banker, kept up a certain level of maintenance, as was observed by the English garden writer Fred Whitsey. He wrote about his visit to Serre de la Madone for *Country Life* magazine in July 1986, describing how "The hedges were trim, the main paths swept, the steps safe to hurry up and down … the garden's old magic still remains." But he also noticed that the unchecked

plant growth threatening to submerge certain areas might soon send the garden into decline.

Indeed, the situation at Serre de la Madone highlighted the plight faced by any garden notable more for its planting than its design or architectural features. While damaged or decayed architectural gardens can often be rebuilt, a highly horticultural garden such as Serre de la Madone relies on constant attention to keep the balance of planting as intended. If that attention lapses, the essence of the planting is gradually lost and the personal vision that inspired the garden becomes obscured. The priority in such cases is to restore the garden in the spirit of its creator, while ensuring it contains a representative selection of the plants for which it was originally renowned.

A campaign was launched to save Serre de la Madone, and succeeded in getting the garden listed as an historic monument. Combined with the threat of housing development, this helped convince the Conservatoire du Littoral to acquire Serre de la Madone in partnership with the city of Menton and the Alpes-Maritimes local government. The garden's restoration has been masterminded since 1999 by distinguished French landscape architect Gilles Clément, known for his work at Parc André Citroën in Paris, and carried out by the head gardener Benoît Bourdeau and his small team of gardeners.

Clément realized that Johnston's garden could never be recreated, even though it had a strong framework of architectural features and trees, because the intricate planting had evolved into a state of semi-wildness. There was, in addition, a lack of written evidence to serve as guidance, because Johnston never wrote about Serre de la Madone, nor was his gardening much written about during his lifetime. Clément's ambition, therefore, was to arrest the process of decay with the minimum interference, to awaken the garden as if it were a sleeping beauty, and to start a new process of development that would both perpetuate the character of the garden in its heyday and illustrate Johnston's gardening skills.

The fabric of the terraces and the flights of steps have been repaired. The complex watering system has also been restored to working order, so that it once again captures and distributes the hillside's plentiful rainfall. Rampant plants have been tamed in order to rescue the weaker plants they were smothering, and also to reveal the garden's underlying vistas and compositions. The most important and rarest plant genera surviving from Johnston's era have been identified for the gardening team to nurture.

Even the manner in which the garden opens to the public deliberately harks back to Johnston's days. As garden writer Louisa Jones explains, Clément wanted visitors to feel plunged into a magic world where they can spend time "almost as if at home, or, better still, as Johnston's guests might have done" (Jones, 2003: 46–7). The garden has been revived in every dimension by combining practical restoration and replanting with sensitive management and control. It has been done with a deliberately light touch, in the full awareness that Johnston's creation cannot be replicated with precision. What can be retained and developed for future generations, however, is a place alive with his spirit and redolent of his talents.

Aberglasney

CARMARTHENSHIRE • WALES

Unlike either Château de Villandry or Serre de la Madone, which are well-known both within France and internationally, Aberglasney has never been a garden of high repute. For more than 500 years it slumbered in obscurity, hidden deep in a beautiful but remote part of rural Wales. The garden evolved over the centuries, with successive owners adding a series of distinct features, and accumulated overlapping layers of history. Then, for much of the twentieth century, house and garden slipped gradually into decline. By the mid-1990s both were derelict.

As this low point was reached, a group of admirers mounted a campaign to save Aberglasney. Quite by chance, their campaign was given the impetus it needed for success by a remarkable turn of events. In 1993, the Ionic columns missing from a Victorian portico that belonged to the front of the house were spotted in a sale of garden statuary at Christie's auction house in London. The columns were sold, and although they were subsequently returned, the controversy sparked by the affair drew some much-needed attention to the plight of Aberglasney. Encouraged by the ensuing offers of both public and private funding, the Aberglasney Restoration Trust was formed in 1995 and was able to purchase the ruined property for £35,000 ($69,478).

The greatest challenge of the work that followed arose from the degree of damage to house and garden, requiring their total restoration. The house was windowless and largely roofless. Inside, it had been wrecked by decades of neglect and vandalism, which had left it stripped of fittings and decoration. In the grounds, walls and paths had been damaged by the uncontained growth of trees and smaller plants, which also obscured the garden's layout and made it difficult to establish the date of architectural features. Weeds, including large colonies of invasive Japanese knotweed (*Fallopia japonica*), populated every area of the garden, and the silted-up pool had disappeared. Penny David, who supported the campaign to save Aberglasney and wrote a book about its history and restoration, describes in graphic terms the state of the Pool Garden: "Wall cappings crumbled as ivy plunged its roots ever deeper into the soft mortar ... Centenarian conifers outgrew their strength and

RIGHT
A new planting scheme
for the Upper Walled
Garden was designed by
Penelope Hobhouse.
Behind it stands the
house, recently
transformed from a
state of utter decay.

BELOW
The ancient Moat
Garden and the sunken
Cloister Garden
immediately in front
of the house are
both reminders of
Aberglasney's
long history as a
dwelling-place.

sickened, or indeed thrived out of all proportion. The level of the pool itself grew ever lower due to damage to its clay lining" (David, 1999: 74).

Looking at Aberglasney today, it is hard to imagine that this scene of advanced decay could ever have existed. The garden has been resurrected without pastiche, resulting in a modern creation faithful to the key details of the past. The garden designer and historian Penelope Hobhouse, who was involved in the design of the new garden, has remarked on how the complex relationship between past and present inevitably affects the process of restoration: "In remaking the garden, we can only see it and the past through modern eyes" (David, 1999: 6).

Aberglasney's history as a dwelling-place stretches back into the mists of the Middle Ages. Possibly the first, enigmatic mention of the garden occurs in a poem written by the fifteenth-century Welsh bard Lewis Glyn Cothi, who spoke of "nine green gardens" surrounding the hall of Rhydderch ap Rhys ("Ode to Rhydderch ap Rhys" quoted in David, 1999: 11). However, it was the purchase of Aberglasney in around 1600 by Anthony Rudd, Bishop of St David's, that would appear to mark the decisive starting point in the garden's history. Archaeological research has confirmed that the garden's most important architectural feature, the Cloister Garden, dates from Rudd's ownership. Located immediately

to the west of the house, it consists of a rectangular court enclosed by arched walkways and overlooked by raised, terraced walks affording views down into the cloister, as well as outwards to the gardens beyond.

Bishop Rudd's descendants remained at Aberglasney until 1710, when the property was sold to a lawyer by the name of Robert Dyer. It was sold once again in 1803, to Thomas Phillips, who made a fortune during a career as a surgeon in the East India Company before returning to England permanently in 1805. His descendants and increasingly distant heirs retained the estate until the 1950s. By then, problems of maintenance and neglect had already crept in, and the property was sold off in parts during 1956. The estate of 810ha (2,000 acres), which for hundreds of years had the house and garden at its centre, ceased to exist. The central complex of house, garden, cottages, and other buildings, with some 28ha (70 acres) of land, was purchased by lawyer John Charles. He remained the owner until 1977 when, in another sale, the property was reduced to 4ha (10 acres), comprising just the main house and garden.

The house, variously remodelled in both eighteenth and nineteenth centuries, sits with the main areas of restored formal gardens below to the south and west. Here, next to the Cloister Garden, are the adjacent enclosures of the Upper Walled Garden and the Kitchen Garden, with the Pool Garden

immediately beyond to the west. Stretching away north from the house is the fascinating Yew Tunnel, and beyond this stands the tall gatehouse, whose date and purpose remain uncertain. To the east is an informal woodland garden called Bishop Rudd's Walk, and other informal areas, known as the Stream Garden and Pigeon House Wood, lie also on the garden's western edge.

The first stage of the restoration involved piecing together the most accurate picture possible of the different areas of the garden when at their zenith. This was done by amassing information from a range of documentary evidence, in particular from the eighteenth and nineteenth centuries. Equally important was the evidence unearthed by exhaustive archaeology, carried out to determine the age of different structures and to uncover the original form of features that had been overlaid during later periods, as was the case with the Cloister Garden.

Once the research was complete, the trust could plan a programme of work for tackling individual areas of the garden. In some cases, most obviously the Yew Tunnel, curbing the dense growth left unchecked for decades was enough to bring the desired result. Photographs taken in the 1950s show that the tunnel was still well-maintained up to that point, but by the time restoration work began, the tunnel had not been pruned for more than 30 years, and its identity was completely submerged. Ancient yew is tough enough to withstand drastic pruning, so the straggling branches could be removed and the new young growth kept in annual check thereafter.

Of the more formal areas, where work started with weed clearance and the reconstruction of walls and other built features, the restored Cloister Garden is without question the

ABOVE
The medley of summer-flowering annuals and perennials grown for cutting also add dashes of colour to the productive planting in the Kitchen Garden.

The austere symmetry
of the restored Cloister
Garden, the site's most
important architectural
feature, represents
the style favoured in
early seventeenth-
century Wales.

project's architectural triumph. As layers of decay were
removed, archaeologists were able to decipher that the original
symmetrical pattern of stonework had been obscured by
masonry added later, much of it dating from the nineteenth
century. With this discovery, made before reconstruction
began, it was possible to date the original garden to within a
few years of 1600. Here was proof in support of the
assumption that the Cloister Garden was a feature typical of
the Renaissance style that flowered briefly in Britain between
the latter years of Elizabeth I's reign and the outbreak of Civil
War in 1642. In a faithful representation of early seventeenth-
century style, the immaculately rebuilt walls, arches, and
walkways today surround a simple pattern of grass beds
divided by gravel paths.

Many eminent garden historians and designers have given
enthusiastic support, some of it hands-on, to the work at

Aberglasney. One of these was Hal Moggridge, a renowned scholar of historical landscapes and founding partner of the garden design and restoration partnership, Colvin and Moggridge. He provided the design for the Pool Garden, where initial work involved digging out the pool itself, and rebuilding its retaining walls before it could be relined and filled with water again. However, in a manner that exemplifies how the restoration has avoided blindly putting back every historical feature, the ruined Victorian vinery that once stood near the pool has not been reconstructed. Penny David has commented on the reason behind the decision: "This is garden reincarnation, not restoration, and there was no question of Aberglasney Restoration Trust's rebuilding an authentic version of the lost structure" (David, 1999: 96). Only the rear, south-facing wall of the vinery survives, and against this Moggridge has designed a long "hot" border combining plants with silver or purple foliage and others with richly coloured flowers.

The design and replanting of the Upper Walled Garden was carried out by Penelope Hobhouse, another keen supporter of the project. She responded to the area's irregular shape with a design of curved, box-edged beds divided by winding gravel paths leading to a central oval lawn. Some of the herbaceous plants chosen for the beds are known to have been cultivated in Britain prior to 1600 and thus deliberately evoke Aberglasney's past. But, as Hobhouse has explained, historical slavery was never part of the plan: "There are no restrictions: some of the plants here are herbaceous border classics, but if we want to use a modern cultivar we go for it. We decided it just had to be beautiful." (David, 1999: 140)

Immediately below the Upper Walled Garden to the west is the smaller, walled Kitchen Garden where a similar, if simpler, pattern of ordered symmetry has been recreated. Its orderliness is faithful to the model of the Victorian kitchen garden, but its design and planting are new. The four geometric, box-edged beds are filled with a mixture of vegetables, herbs, and flowers. Over the path along one side stretches a new crab-apple tunnel, and beneath the boundary wall on another there is now a mixed border. Against the stone walls, fruit trees are trained between buttresses of evergreen Portugal laurel (*Prunus lusitanica*).

In the more informal areas towards the eastern and western boundaries of the garden, the hand of restoration has been gentler, restricted to remaking paths, removing overgrown trees and vegetation and adding collections of small woodlanders, such as trilliums and primulas, that thrive in shaded conditions. From the garden's perimeters visitors can enjoy views out over the countryside of the Towy Valley and to nearby Grongar Hill. These spectacular views have been part of Aberglasney's appeal for centuries and are a reminder of how this Herculean restoration project has successfully rebuilt and rejuvenated a garden while also retaining unbroken links with its past. This was the key objective from the outset, as Penny David confirms: "'Restoration' was in the name of the trust, but it did not mean that the mansion or its gardens were to be returned to some point in their history and held there in aspic" (David, 1999: 176).

By taking such an unashamedly forward-looking approach, the Aberglasney Restoration Trust has not only managed to see through a highly ambitious restoration programme, but it has also met the even more daunting challenge of providing the garden with a viable future. A corps of enthusiastic volunteers, a continuing supply of donations, and a large audience of visitors are the life-blood of a garden's long-term health, once restoration has been completed. Aberglasney's well-publicized attractions are strong enough to draw in visitors for many years to come and will ensure a new phase of bustling life to rival the centuries of quiet development that the garden enjoyed in the past.

OPPOSITE
Although it had
been neglected
for more than 30 years,
the ancient Yew Tunnel
was one of the easier
aspects of Aberglasney
to restore.

ABOVE
A restored path in
Bishop Rudd's Wood,
one of the woodland
areas that contrast so
well with the formal
gardens immediately
around the house.

ICONS OF THEIR AGE

Garden fashions have changed inexorably over the centuries, inspiring the creation of new gardens, often at the cost of pre-existing designs that were deemed outdated. An obvious example is the informal English Landscape style that was influential in the eighteenth century, which swept away formal gardens as it spread through Europe. Similarly, when the fussy style of England's High Victorian period fell out of fashion, many of its most impressive examples were destroyed. In recent decades, however, garden restorations have helped to revive our appreciation and understanding of neglected garden styles.

Lednice and Valtice

MORAVIA · CZECH REPUBLIC

Towards the end of its heyday in the early twentieth century, the enormous park of the combined Lednice and Valtice estates extended to some 200ha (494 acres) and was one of the largest designed landscapes in Europe. The two neighbouring estates, located in southern Moravia (now part of the Czech Republic), were linked by avenues of lime trees, and their joint park was modified over the course of many years. This landscape encapsulates the desire to create an idealized vision of nature that dominated garden design in this region of central Europe between the eighteenth and nineteenth centuries.

The upheavals of World War I overshadowed the estates for decades, and it was not until after World War II that the Czech government stepped in to restore some of the park's surviving ornamental buildings. In 1996 UNESCO named the landscape as a World Heritage Site, bringing international recognition of the park's importance, and also security for the successive fashions represented by the formal gardens created close to the twin châteaux.

The history of the park and gardens is closely connected with the rise of the wealthy, powerful Liechtenstein family, who owned land around the village of Lednice from the thirteenth century onwards. The Liechtensteins were involved in the politics of the Holy Roman Empire, acting as advisers to the ruling Habsburg dynasty, and were made dukes in the late sixteenth century. Their fortunes rose higher still when the head of the family became the first Prince of Liechtenstein (Karl I) in 1608. Not surprisingly, they developed their estates in a suitably ambitious manner, and as fashions changed so did their residences. In this way, the treasures of one period were often replaced or overlaid by those of the next. The grand baroque garden of the late seventeenth and early eighteenth centuries was swept away by the English-style landscape park that was developed and expanded into the nineteenth century. Then, in the mid-nineteenth century, the Lednice château and part of its garden were remodelled in neo-Gothic style, bringing yet another strong influence into play.

When the Liechtensteins began embellishing Lednice in the seventeenth century, Moravia was a prosperous province where baroque architecture and gardens were flowering, just as they were in neighbouring Bohemia and Slovakia. The second Prince of Liechtenstein, Karl Eusebius, was devoted to the arts and built on the work begun by his father, who he succeeded in 1627 at the age of 16. He made Lednice into a sumptuous

LEFT
Seen from within Lednice Castle, this vista towards the park was photographed in the nineteenth century, when the Italianate garden was still new. A series of hedged enclosures was laid out facing the conservatory.

OPPOSITE
The joint Lednice-Valtice Park was shaped over a span of 300 years. This view indicates the scale of the landscape and how the flat, marshy site lent itself to the creation of large lakes.

baroque château to the design of two Italian architects, Giovanni Giacomo Tencalla and Francesco Caratti. The surrounding baroque gardens, equally elaborate, were influenced by Caratti, in particular, as well as the Italian gardener Manini, who is recorded to have been at Lednice from the 1650s. The gardens comprised an intricate arrangement of scrollwork parterres, green theatres, and decorative screens formed by belts of trees. A fountain of tiered shells, swans, and dolphins survives from this era.

The château was considerably altered during the early eighteenth century by Domenico Martinelli; the influential Austrian architect, Johann Bernhard Fischer von Erlach, was responsible for the addition of the enormous stable wing. It was also during this period, in 1712–21, that avenues of trees were planted to link Lednice with the Valtice estate. Greater changes followed in the late eighteenth century, influenced by neoclassicism and the early English Landscape movement: most of the Italian-inspired gardens vanished in favour of a Romantic park. Since the land around Lednice is flat, low-lying, and prone to flooding, the engineer Joseph Uebelacher was called in to

create a series of rivers and ditches along which water would drain into ponds and lakes. The pump-house that drove the system was disguised within a building decorated in Islamic style.

By the late eighteenth century, many such ornamental buildings had been created for the park that was to become such an icon of its type. The first group was designed by the architect Joseph Hardtmuth, and the most memorable of his buildings to survive is the 61m (200ft) high minaret overlooking one of the lakes. Hardtmuth also designed the obelisk and two picturesque ruins (a "Roman" aqueduct and a medieval-style castle); these can still be seen, but his Chinese pavilion, Dutch fisherman's house, and classical temple have disappeared. The increasingly extensive landscape into which these monuments were placed was at the same time being embellished with plants, in a scheme masterminded by Ignac Holle. He was assisted in his choice of native and exotic trees by the botanist Joseph van der Schott (whose son became director of the Imperial Habsburg Gardens at Schönbrunn in Vienna).

The park continued to be expanded and altered into the early nineteenth century, when the architect Fanti enlarged the

OPPOSITE
The long, cast-iron
conservatory at Lednice,
seen here beyond the
restored parterre,
replaced the baroque
orangery when extensive
changes were made to
park and garden in the
nineteenth century.

BELOW
An imposing neo-
Gothic facade for the
château at Lednice
was commissioned in
the 1850s, to replace
the lavish baroque
original built for the
Liechtenstein family
by Italian architects.

LEFT AND ABOVE
The most striking
building in the park
is the tall minaret
overlooking the lake.
It was one of a series of
ornamental structures
designed in the late
eighteenth century
by architect
Joseph Hardtmuth.

OPPOSITE
The nineteenth-century
parterres were restored
to their original layout
after the Czech
government gained
ownership of the estate
in the 1940s. The
combination of formal
gardens and landscape
park is recognized as a
UNESCO World
Heritage Site.

system of drainage and water features, notably with the addition of the largest lake. Covering more than 30ha (74 acres), it extended into the Valtice estate and was shaped into a series of inlets and islands joined by bridges. Further buildings, designed by the Viennese architect Joseph Kornhäusel (who also remodelled the house in neoclassical style), were sited around the park, including the impressive, classically inspired triumphal arch known as the Rendezvous or Temple of Diana. The architect Johann Karl Engel also contributed designs for the belvedere and Temple of the Three Graces.

By the mid-nineteenth century, tastes had changed once again, and the Viennese architect Georg Wingelmüller was commissioned to refashion the Lednice château in the neo-Gothic style that he had studied while in England. He died in 1855, before the work could be completed, but his design for the château has largely survived to this day. Wingelmüller was also responsible for the last building added to the park: the neo-Gothic Chapel of St Hubert, hidden deep in the woods.

Just as Victorian England had provided the architectural model for Wingelmüller's alterations to the house, so, too, did it provide the inspiration for the last additions to the gardens immediately surrounding the two châteaux. The historicist blend of Elizabethan and Italianate formality echoed the style of the garden created in 1840 by Sir Charles Barry, the English architect and garden designer, at Trentham in Staffordshire. Since it had become fashionable in the mid-nineteenth century

to interpose a formal garden between the house and the naturally inspired parkland beyond, Barry laid out three shallow terraces leading down to the park designed in the previous century by Lancelot "Capability" Brown. Like Lednice, Trentham was created from a flat, marshy site. Italianate statuary and balustrades were mixed with Elizabethan-style topiary and hedging, along with colourful Victorian bedding in patterned flowerbeds.

Other changes were made in a more forward-looking spirit, making use of new technology and discoveries. The conservatory completed in 1848 to replace Lednice's surviving baroque-period orangery was designed by English architect P H Devien, who used the revolutionary cast-iron, domed construction that would be perfected most notably in the Palm House at Kew Gardens, near London. The parkland joining the two estates was enlivened in this period with a host of exotic, newly introduced evergreens and flowering trees. From North America came Colorado spruce (*Picea pungens*), western red cedar (*Thuja plicata*), black locust (*Robinia pseudoacacia*), and flowering Osage orange (*Maclura pomifera*), while China provided the Amur cork tree (*Phellodendron amurense*).

By the beginning of the twentieth century, the Lednice-Valtice landscape was one of the largest and most complex in Europe, having evolved over 300 years under the stewardship of a single family. While the formal gardens had been altered to reflect the latest fashion, resulting in layers of different styles

superimposed on one another, the parkland underwent a more continuous development. Embellishing the natural landscape, successive generations of Liechtensteins added lakes, exotic plants, and varied monuments according to the taste of the period, leading towards the creation of a harmonious whole.

No further development took place at this point, and in the years after World War II the major question was one of resources for the necessary maintenance and restoration. Control of the property had been ceded to the Czech government in the 1940s, and, realizing the significance of the landscape, it initiated a programme of conservation focused on the main houses and ornamental buildings. In 1992, the site's status was formalized as a Monument Zone by the Czech Ministry of Culture, and four years later it became a UNESCO World Heritage Site.

In its assessment, UNESCO described Lednice as "an exceptional example of a planned cultural landscape, made more impressive by the wealth and diversity of its cultural and natural elements". Other great European gardens, such as Versailles in France or Sintra in Portugal, "may rival it in specific qualities, but none compares in terms of its combination of features" (UNESCO Evaluation, 1995). Although only echoes of the original rich, baroque architecture and gardens remain, the succeeding neoclassical, picturesque, Romantic, Italianate, and neo-Gothic influences have survived. Stimulated by international recognition, the Czech authorities are continuing restoration work to conserve Lednice-Valtice in all its remarkable diversity.

ABOVE
This monumental colonnade, built on a hill above the city of Valtice, provides a platform for far-reaching views towards the Carpathian Mountains and into Austria.

OPPOSITE
The palace of Valtice has retained its long, classically elegant eighteenth-century facade, looking out towards the enormous surrounding park that it shares with Lednice.

Brodsworth Hall

YORKSHIRE • ENGLAND

In October 1985, an article about Brodsworth Hall appeared in the English *Country Life* magazine, written by noted social and architectural historian Mark Girouard. He was concerned about the hall's uncertain future and drew attention to its historical importance. He described it as the most complete surviving example of a Victorian country house in England: "complete because it is a stylistic unity, built, decorated, furnished and landscaped between 1861 and 1870".

The house was designed by Italian architect G M Casentini for Charles Thellusson, who inherited the estate in 1859. His ancestors belonged to a Huguenot family of bankers from Switzerland who had arrived in England during the eighteenth century and acquired the Brodsworth estate, located near Doncaster in Yorkshire, which they subsequently extended to thousands of acres. The original house was replaced during the 1860s by Casentini's neoclassical edifice, built with limestone quarried on the estate, although the elaborate adornments that Casentini envisaged for the house exterior, including a conservatory, were not all executed. It is probable that he never came to England, and the construction of the house was overseen by an English architect, Philip Wilkinson.

At the time of Girouard's article, Brodsworth Hall was the home of Mrs Grant-Dalton, an octogenarian widow who had

OPPOSITE
The main flower garden lies to the west of the house, beyond a broad croquet lawn. Neoclassical in style, the house was built in the 1860s using limestone quarried at Brodsworth.

BELOW
A similar view of the flower garden taken in the late nineteenth century shows the evergreen shrubbery at its intended height. The exotic coniferous trees, however, are still juvenile.

cared for the house for half a century. The estate had been inherited by her husband and passed to her after his death in 1952. However, sale and dispersal of the property seemed inevitable because no member of the family planned to live at the hall after Mrs Grant-Dalton's death, and the lack of money to form a sufficient endowment made it unlikely that the National Trust would agree to take on the house and garden.

Although the interior of the house had retained a faded period accuracy into the 1980s, decades of inactivity meant that the Italianate gardens, laid out to complement the house, had all but ceased to exist. Similar gardens had been made at Trentham in Staffordshire and Osborne House on the Isle of Wight, but their derivative style became deeply unfashionable as the Victorian era came to an end. From the 1880s, the Arts and Crafts Movement, with its emphasis on the principles of medieval craftsmanship, followed by the influence of William Robinson and Gertrude Jekyll, took English garden design to a more natural style, albeit still set within a formal structure.

In the event, it was English Heritage that undertook to restore Brodsworth Hall. It recognized the value of the 6ha (15-acre) garden, which illustrates how a style that was once the height of fashion had fallen from favour during subsequent generations, and had only been preserved in part due to the conservative affection of its owners. By the 1990s, support for an authentic recreation of the garden had grown, and, with public and private funding in place, English Heritage began a restoration programme that was to last for more than a decade.

The original garden had a classically formal layout, as befitted such an unashamedly Italianate house, within which there were flower gardens, generous shrubberies planted with evergreen species that would tolerate the chilly Yorkshire climate (and stand out as fashionable novelties during the late nineteenth century), and a selection of fine, mature trees. The monkey puzzle tree (*Araucaria araucana*) to the west of the house, located in the restored flower garden beyond the croquet lawn, is a survivor from the 1860s layout, and venerable cedars of Lebanon (*Cedrus libani*) adorn the broad, curving lawn opposite the east entrance of the house.

Apart from these ancient trees, and a tiered fountain sculpted from Italian marble, little remained of the garden's past glories by the time restoration began. However, research uncovered written evidence that was put together with the results of an archaeological investigation, and this enabled English Heritage to establish the position of the parterre-like

RIGHT
A tiered fountain of Italian marble is the central focal point in the flower garden, where the restored parterre of flowerbeds is filled with pelargoniums for summer. Victorian monkey puzzle trees tower above.

BELOW
Undergrowth that had
choked the woodland
walks was cleared away
during the 1990s
restoration, opening up
views to this classical
statue. Also, the garden's
surviving ornaments
were carefully cleaned.

flowerbeds and recreate them complete with structural clipped yew at the corners. The beds are now filled with impressive seasonal bedding schemes that faithfully represent the Victorian art of this labour-intensive form of planting. A bright late-spring display of tulips combined with plants such as daisies, hyacinths, and polyanthus-type primulas, is replaced for summer with a blaze of colour from massed pelargoniums. The cultivars used would all have been available in the nineteenth century.

Another consciously period planting feature is the long border of dark-red dahlias ("Bishop of Llandaff") that provides rich late-summer colour in front of a stretch of sombre green yew hedge. There is also an an extensive collection of the repeat-flowering, damask-type Portland roses so favoured by the Victorians; named after the Duchess of Portland, who is thought to have brought them to England from Italy, they have strongly perfumed double flowers.

Along the main facade of the house stretches a broad terrace, from which three parallel flights of stone steps lead down to the lawn and superb views to the parkland beyond. Now that the white marble urns and figures of recumbent whippets have been returned to their original positions beside the steps, and the yew hedge around the lawn has regained its neat symmetry with niches containing statues, this area of the garden again corresponds to the house's architectural style.

LEFT
When English Heritage took on Brodsworth Hall, this fountain was one of the few reminders of the garden's Italianate splendour. In this photograph, it is surrounded by a well-tended but much-altered flower garden.

BELOW
The main challenges at Brodsworth were to reverse structural damage (such as to the roof of this small temple) and to tackle the tangle of near-wild vegetation.

A striking contrast in atmosphere lies beyond the main flower garden, to the west of the house, where a woodland garden offers meandering walks among ornamental shrubs. It had become overgrown by the 1980s and needed careful clearance before the paths could be restored and a choice selection of plants added. The woodland leads on to the garden's most intriguing feature, made on the site of the old limestone quarry. It has been replanted in classic Victorian style as a fernery, displaying a private collection of historic fern cultivars that was donated to Brodsworth Hall in 2000. The ferns have established well in the damp shade here, with the bonus of added moisture provided by the original 1860s cascade.

A Gothic-style pavilion was one of the few features to have survived from the previous, eighteenth-century garden, but in order to complete the period feel of the restoration, it was adapted to reflect Victorian tastes. With the addition of a thatched roof and deep eaves, it now resembles the Swiss cottage that Queen Victoria erected in the gardens of Frogmore House, her retreat near Windsor Castle in Berkshire. Given the quantity of affluent English households for whom decorative Italianate formality would have been the ultimate fashionable goal from 1850 until around 1890, it is a reflection of the fall in popularity of this garden style that so few examples have survived.

The success of the restoration at Brodsworth Hall is to have preserved such a complete period piece, as Mark Girouard had urged in his 1985 article. Brodsworth's great quality as a High-Victorian garden is that it was not diluted by earlier designs or later alterations. Its great good fortune is for enough key features to have survived so that conscientious restoration could produce such a delightful and historically important replica.

Château de Marqueyssac

DORDOGNE • FRANCE

The restoration at the Château de Marqueyssac in south-western France has brought back to life one of the country's most extraordinary gardens. At the same time, it has served to champion a style of gardening that suffered from neglect in the aftermath of World World II, when interest in its intricate planting and design dwindled. Even though Marqueyssac was not well known before its revival in the mid-1990s, it is now one of the most popular gardens in the Dordogne region, due to the winning combination of an unforgettable location and a wonderfully individual style.

The château sits perched on a rocky limestone outcrop, nearly 150m (490ft) above the winding river Dordogne, with panoramic views to landmarks such as the brooding fortress of Castelnaud, the Château de Fayrac, and the Romanesque chapel at Cénac-et-Saint-Julien. As can well be imagined, this imposing site has been occupied for hundreds of years. The Marqueyssac family built the first château here during the fourteenth century. In 1692, the property was purchased by Bertrand Vernet de Marqueyssac, who commissioned a design for the gardens laid out on the terraces around the château. The designer, named Porcher, was found through an adviser to King Louis XIV in the nearby town of Sarlat, and was a pupil of André Le Nôtre (who designed the royal gardens at Versailles). At the end of the the eighteenth century, the château was destroyed by fire, and shortly afterwards the present edifice was built by François de Cerval, who was able to retain from the old building only the circular staircase tower in the centre of the main facade.

The Marqueyssac estate was cultivated primarily for grape production, and although successive members of the de Cerval

OPPOSITE
A wonderful patchwork
of clipped box once
again fills the garden
behind the delightful
eighteenth-century
Château de Marqueyssac.
Many of the original box
plants responded well to
hard pruning followed
by careful reshaping.

LEFT
Pine trees shade the
domes and swirls of
evergreen boxwood.
From this terrace, and
throughout the garden,
lookouts marked by
stone urns and vases
provide extensive views
over the valley beyond.

ABOVE
Mist rising from the
river Dordogne adds to
the magical atmosphere
of this whimsical garden,
created by Julien de
Cerval in the 1860s. He
admired the Renaissance
gardens he had seen
while a soldier in Italy.

family made slight alterations to the terraced gardens, they remained largely the same for nearly 150 years. Within the 22ha (54 acres) or so that surrounded the château, an avenue, or *grande allée*, was laid out in the eighteenth century, leading from the boxwood terraces to the viewpoint of the belvedere. There was a park where the owners exercised their horses, but this had become a wilderness by the time a second garden of note was created in the second half of the nineteenth century.

It was Julien de Cerval who set about remodelling the garden after he inherited the estate in 1861. He drew inspiration from the time he had spent in Italy as captain of the Papal Zouaves, an international army of volunteers formed in defence of the Papal States and active there until the Unification of Italy in 1870. He took as his model those Italian Renaissance gardens, in particular the smaller ones sited on steep hillsides, that made conventional use of some containing

symmetry yet also showed bravado in their use of plants, especially evergreens.

De Cerval filled the irregularly shaped terraces and enclosures around the château with tens of thousands of evergreen box plants that were clipped into dramatically organic, abstract shapes such as domes, swirls, and columns. The use of box was extended to form neat clipped hedging along the paths throughout the parkland, which was itself renovated by a process of clearance and new planting. It is estimated that de Cerval planted a total of 6km (3.7 miles) of boxwood, but he also added some more colourful flourishes: evergreen, rusty-barked strawberry tree (*Arbutus unedo*), pink-flowered Judas tree (*Cercis siliquastrum*), and carpets of small, autumn-flowering Neapolitan cyclamen (*Cyclamen hederifolium*).

Every vantage point was used to full effect, with the addition of balustraded lookouts and seats. Progress through the garden, either in the open, box-filled terraces or along paths shaded by evergreen oaks and pines, leads to the climax of the belvedere, which commands one of the most memorable of all the garden's viewpoints. In certain parts of the garden, de Cerval erected simple domed drystone shelters, of the sort that are a characteristic feature of the Dordogne landscape. There are echoes, too, of his connection with the Vatican: the "Pope's Seat" was positioned to commemorate a visit by the Bishop of Mantua, who went on to become Pope Pius X in 1903.

After de Cerval's death in 1893, Marqueyssac passed to his daughter and son-in-law, and in 1948 the fabric of the château was partly secured when it was listed in the register of French historical monuments. Yet the gardens were not included, and they became neglected in the years following World War II. No doubt the need to clip thousands of metres of boxwood influenced their decline, as did a lack of interest in their elaborate style. By the time the gardens were recognized as a listed site in 1969, the patterns of boxwood adorning the terraces had all but disappeared.

The Marqueyssac estate was divided and sold off in four sections in 1994. The quarter containing the château, with its surrounding garden and park, was leased to the Kléber Rossillon company, owner of the neighbouring Château de Castelnaud. Having already restored Castelnaud and earned a reputation as a champion of France's architectural and garden heritage, the company undertook a year-long restoration at Marqueyssac. The

OPPOSITE, TOP
A wooded bank overlooks one of the paths on the shaded north side of the garden, where birch trees, limes, and hornbeams grow.

OPPOSITE, BOTTOM
Neat box hedges behind lavender now line the *grande allée*, an avenue that extends through the garden and ends at the breathtaking view given by the belvedere.

LEFT
Plants cling to the steep limestone hillside below one of Marqueyssac's enormous retaining walls. Its dramatic position contributes to the popularity of the garden, which opened to the public in 1997.

chief goal within the garden was to reinstate the patterns of box on the terraces and to return the hedged walkways and avenues to their former neat, shaded solitude. In testament to the toughness of box, many of the old plants were retained and carefully pruned back to a size from which they could then be clipped into shape. There are some 150,000 individual boxwood plants in the garden today, trimmed by hand twice a year (in early summer and autumn) by the team of four gardeners.

Other parts of the garden brought back to life include the *grande allée* leading to the belvedere, and the early twentieth-century addition of an area devoted to exotic-looking Mediterranean plants. Stone urns and vases have been replaced on the walls and balustrades, which together contain the terraces and frame views into the landscape beyond, and the network of winding paths are once again clear and gravelled. The gardens were opened to the public for the first time in March 1997 and have since grown rapidly in popularity.

Marqueyssac is an overpoweringly romantic garden, its atmosphere heightened by the contrast of the green-hued boxwood and the cream and grey tones of the château. The magic is even stronger when a dense mist rises from the river

and forms a carpet around the garden, while blue sky and sunlight are visible above. At moments such as this, when time seems suspended, you can truly enter into the spirit of the place and appreciate the more whimsical aspects of Julien de Cerval's garden-making. He wrote a poem in honour of the Asiatic earth goddess Cybele, who represented the force of nature and was a protectress of wild animals, and displayed it in the garden for all to read. This tradition is perpetuated by poetical signs placed around the garden for the enjoyment of today's visitors.

It is clear from what de Cerval planted that he understood the contrasting microclimates and natural vegetation on the two sides of the peninsula on which the château stands. The sunny and craggy southern side is clothed with tough, Mediterranean plants, such as evergreen holm oaks, Corsican pines, junipers, and fig trees. The shadier and cooler northern side shelters deciduous birch, lime, and hornbeam trees. For most visitors, however, it is not the horticultural merits of Marqueyssac that leave the greatest impression, nor the achievements of the recent restoration. Above all, people remember the remarkable location, the swirling boxwood terraces, and an atmosphere that vividly recalls the garden's fascinating past.

OPPOSITE
AND RIGHT
The paths and avenues
that lead through
wooded glades are lined
with a large number
of the garden's total
150,000 boxwood
plants. The lack of labour
needed to trim them
twice a year contributed
to the garden's decline
in the 1950s.

HEALING TIME

Some gardens have the good fortune to remain in the hands of a single family, or to change hands only infrequently, but the simple passage of time can still create the need for restoration. The most ephemeral of gardens are those whose character is defined largely by planting schemes that require consistent maintenance. Architectural gardens have greater permanence, but they, too, can lose their essential qualities as the years pass. Over time, even gentle decline can be detrimental to historically important gardens. Their glory days can be revived, however, through sensitive restoration.

Villa Farnese

CAPRAROLA • ITALY

The mighty Villa Farnese, which dominates the village of Caprarola and views across the Lazio countryside towards Rome, has long been acknowledged as one of the foremost architectural and garden-design achievements of the Italian Renaissance. Recent restoration work, carried out by the Italian state to repair the inevitable effects of age, has needed to be especially sensitive to the distinguished historical background of the site.

The original fortress was built in the early sixteenth century for Cardinal Alessandro Farnese, who later became Pope Paul III. He commissioned the architects Baldassare Peruzzi and Antonio da Sangallo the younger, who devised a pentagonal plan on a monumental scale. During the 1550s the fortress was transformed into a palazzo for the Pope's nephew, Cardinal Alessandro Farnese II, by Giacomo Barozzi da Vignola, one of the leading architects of the Italian Renaissance. Alterations

were made to the building in the late sixteenth and seventeenth centuries by Giacomo del Duca and Girolamo Rainaldi, but the present appearance of the palazzo – and its garden – owe most to Vignola's work.

Vignola created two large, walled enclosures that were positioned along adjacent sides of the pentagonal building and were reached by crossing balustraded bridges over a dry moat. These formal gardens, each 70 sq m (753 sq ft) in size, were accessed from inside the palazzo by doors on the main floor, or *piano nobile*, and were designed to make the maximum impression when viewed from the windows of the grand reception rooms. Named the Winter Garden and the Summer Garden, both were square in outline and subdivided into four symmetrical compartments. Within these, patterns formed by clipped box hedges were surrounded by ranks of statues between cypress trees. The stone statues are herms, a

LEFT
A seventeenth-century watercolour of Villa Farnese shows how the two walled gardens were laid out with grand parterres. They were designed to be viewed from the windows of the main reception rooms within the pentagonal palazzo.

OPPOSITE
Vignola, the celebrated Renaissance architect, is responsible for the superb *catena d'acqua* (an artificial cascade) that forms the centrepiece of a secret garden located away from the villa. Water tumbles down the central sculpted cascade between gently descending ramps of steps.

form in which portraits of male and female heads are displayed on square stone pillars.

The gardens could only ever provide a degree of formal complement to the overwhelming architecture of the vast palazzo, whereas Vignola proved in other garden commissions, most memorably the nearby Villa Lante at Bagnaia, that his real genius was in the proportional unity of a building with its garden. At Caprarola, Vignola displayed the full force of his skills with the ornamental pavilion known as the Casino del Piacere (House of Pleasure) and adjoining *giardino segreto*, or secret garden, which he designed for Cardinal Alessandro Farnese II in 1560. An important element of Renaissance design, the secret garden was typically an enclosed space next to the house, providing an intimate contrast to the main gardens. While it may appear grand when seen out of context, Vignola's *casino*

and its garden are small and secret compared to the main villa. The harmonious composition of his *giardino segreto* has been praised as "one of the greatest masterpieces of Renaissance art" (Hobhouse, 1998: 101), and it has also been suggested that "no other garden in Italy, or probably in the world, contains a surprise as ravishing as this" (Masson, 1987: 141).

The Casino del Piacere was the cardinal's haven from public life; only invited guests had access. It is reached along a path from the Summer Garden, winding for 400m (1,300ft) through the *parchetto*, a woodland of pine trees, beeches, evergreen oaks, and sweet chestnuts. Visitors emerge at the lower level of the secret garden, where they are greeted by a dazzling water cascade, or *catena d'acqua*. Water tumbling from a large, arched pool cascades down a series of basins that are carved to represent interlinking dolphins and lie between twin flights of wide, shallow steps. The whole construction is given dramatic perspective by the high, decorated walls on either side. At the bottom of the steps, the water pours from a large scalloped shell, carved from stone, into a circular pool enlivened by a single jet fountain.

Above the *catena d'acqua*, the water appears to be supplied by a pair of enormous stone figures, depicting river gods, who lie recumbent on either side of the central vista and pour water into a huge urn. This combination is known as the Fontana dei Fiumi, or Fountain of the Rivers, behind which curving flights

Changes in level at Villa Farnese were executed with architectural flair, as was the decoration to stonework both in the main parterres and in the *giardino segreto*.

ABOVE
No longer a scene of romantic decay, the parterre gardens have been restored in detail to their sixteenth-century appearance. The sharp lines of the replanted box hedges are accentuated on a winter's day.

RIGHT
High, decorated walls give dramatic perspective to the cascade and lower pool of the secret garden: an example of the unity of architecture, decoration, and water for which Vignola is noted.

of steps lead up to the highest terrace, situated immediately in front of the central triple-arched loggia of the *casino*. The upper garden was created in the 1620s, around 50 years after Vignola's death, by the Mannerist architect Girolamo Rainaldi. He worked for the Farnese family for many years and carried out a number of commissions for them in the village of Caprarola, including a church and several fountains. Vignola's terrace was given a pattern of box hedges and is most memorable for the surrounding rows of stone herms carved by Pietro Bernini.

Vignola's munificent patron, Cardinal Alessandro Farnese II, died in 1589. He bequeathed his estates, including Villa Farnese, to the Farnese dukes of Parma, who remained in ownership until the eighteenth century. The removal of the cardinal's fabulous art collection to other family homes signalled a declining interest in Villa Farnese, and the gardens entered a long period of neglect. In the mid-nineteenth century, with the unification of Italy under King Victor Emmanuel, the palazzo was nominated as an official residence for the heir to the newly forged kingdom of Italy. However, even though Villa Farnese was effectively under state care, it received little attention. Details of the garden's layout were lost beneath overgrown plants; architectural features and statuary suffered, and water ceased to flow.

When American novelist Edith Wharton visited Villa Farnese in the early twentieth century, the architecture of the large walled gardens beside the palazzo, including staircases, herms, and grotto, was still in place. But the parterre had all but disappeared, as had the parterres and flower gardens on the upper terrace by the *casino*, and on the terrace below, the steps on either side of the water cascade were obscured with grass. The grand formality of Rainaldi's parterres and the delicate composition of Vignola's *giardino segreto* meant that the impact of both were diminished by the long process of ageing.

Decay can sometimes have its own special beauty, as described of the gardens of the nearby Villa d'Este in Tivoli by Isa Bella Barsali, which had also been neglected during the nineteenth century: "no longer the place which delighted its original creators … it is an altogether different garden, a romantic wood where you stumble across architectural fragments like islands with fountains gushing from them" (Mosser & Teyssot, 1990: 528). As alluring as this scene may have been, the Villa d'Este was nevertheless restored, and neither was romantic abandon considered a suitable fate for Villa Farnese, which has become a private summer residence available to the president of Italy.

Instead, judicious restoration has ensured that the overall brilliance and the superb details of Vignola's design can be enjoyed by visitors today. The main parterres of the Winter and Summer gardens have been reinstated, and similar replanting has taken place on the upper terrace of the *casino* garden. Individual stone herms have been restored where necessary, and the steps flanking the *catena d'acqua* have been cleared of vegetation and can play their intended role within the ornamental scheme. In keeping with its historic significance as one of the most ingenious creations of the Italian Renaissance, the garden is once again visible in its dramatic entirety.

RIGHT
The upper terrace of the secret garden surrounds an ornamental pavilion that was built in 1560 as a refuge from the public life of the main villa. This photograph was taken years before restoration began.

Carmen de los Martires

GRANADA • SPAIN

From the imperceptible moment it is set in motion, the gradual process of decline in a once-glorious garden can continue for decades. It was already under way by the 1920s in the Carmen de los Martires, a terraced garden created around a nineteenth-century villa in Granada, southern Spain. The state of the garden was observed by two American authors, who commented in 1924: "It is a mid-Victorian interpretation of Andalusian, most interesting for its orange terraces and the use of potted plants along the parapets. In recent years it has become quite overgrown and formless, but many beautiful little spots can still be found" (Byne & Byne, 1924: 179). It was not until 50 years later, when the garden's very existence was threatened by plans to build a hotel, that its future was assured and the steady decline was at last halted. Now owned by the city, it has been restored and opened to the public.

Carmen de los Martires is set on the southern slopes of the hill also occupied by the celebrated Alhambra Generalife Gardens, with breathtaking views out over the city of Granada. A stone cross put up near the entrance to the property at the start of the twentieth century hints at the history of the site, as

does the name "Carmen de los Martires". Meaning "Garden of the Martyrs", the name is a reference to the Christian martyrs killed here in the fourteenth century by the Moorish rulers of Granada. After the city was reconquered by the Spanish in 1492, Queen Isabella I put up a monument to the martyrs, and a Carmelite convent was built on the site during the sixteenth century. The terraced structure of the gardens dates partly from this period.

In 1845, after the convent was destroyed, the property was sold into private ownership, and shortly afterwards General Don Carlos Calderón built the neoclassical villa that can still be seen today. The gardens were made principally at the turn of the twentieth century by his successor, Hubert Meersmans, a wealthy Belgian businessman who came to settle in Granada. The site was blessed with a plentiful supply of water, fed into the garden along an aqueduct, and Meersmans harnessed this to create a variety of fountains, pools, and grottoes. He also added an array of statuary and urns, creating rich combinations with choice trees such as evergreen *Magnolia grandiflora*; *Arbutus unedo*, with red, strawberry-like fruits; London plane trees (*Platanus x hispanica*); and various flowering horse chestnuts. The work begun by Meersmans was continued by the Duke del Infantado, who became the property's new owner in 1930.

Carmen de los Martires holds a special place among the gardens of Granada, being both the city's largest garden and also quite different in character to the famous Moorish gardens at the Alhambra. Now that it has been restored, the garden clearly shows the original nineteenth-century combination of picturesque and neoclassical styles. Water is the recurring theme that binds the different elements together, most notably on the terraces. The tone is set for visitors from the moment they step through the entrance, where they are greeted by a grotto shrouded in ferns and decorated with statues of water nymphs, and it continues through to the lake and stream located away from the villa, on the garden's largest, upper terraced level. There are formal circular and rectangular pools with calm, reflecting surfaces, in addition to movement from splashing fountains and dripping grottoes. Beyond a colonnade next to the house lies a terrace with spectacular views over the city; it is almost filled by a single canal, the stillness of which contrasts with the constantly flowing cascade against the wall at one end.

The water features combine with the planting to great effect. On one terrace, for example, a pool adorned with a statue of Neptune stands at the heart of a parterre delineated by clipped box. The pool is planted with white-flowered arum lilies (*Zantedeschia aethiopica*) and surrounded by roses and orange trees, while towering above it are Canary Island date palms (*Phoenix canariensis*) and evergreen magnolias. In a separate area, a pool containing a tall, three-tiered fountain is concealed beneath the spreading canopy of a grove of palm trees.

Some of the garden's original trees, planted in the late nineteenth century, can be seen beside the naturally shaped lake and on the island at its centre. The lake is the most clearly romantic feature in the garden; an arched bridge leads over the water to the island, where a secret grotto awaits discovery.

LEFT
Tall cypress trees form a dramatic backdrop to this long terrace, which provides wonderful views over the city. The terraced structure of the garden dates back to the Carmelite convent built here in the sixteenth century.

OPPOSITE
Spanish neoclassicism is the most evident influence on this terrace, where Neptune stands at the centre of a formal pool surrounded by sentinel classical statues. Other areas of the garden are more picturesque in style.

Meersmans planned this area as an exotic woodland filled with ornamental evergreen and flowering species, and hidden among the trees he placed a surprise clearing where classical statues stand, with great presence, around the perimeter of a large, circular pool. On the garden's lower levels, a number of the terraces are enclosed by tall hedges of clipped cypresses, as originally intended, and the dramatic contrast created between these enclosures and other spaces with open views accounts for much of the garden's theatrical appeal.

Certain parts of the garden were destroyed in the 1970s, when the estate was bought by a property developer and preparations were made to construct a luxury hotel. Areas of woodland suffered the most damage, and the felling of trees at Carmen de los Martires caused such outrage in Granada, a city with one of the finest garden heritages in Europe, that the municipal authorities stepped in and acquired the whole site before any construction work began. The threat of destruction fortunately led the way to the garden's salvation: careful restoration began in the mid-1980s and continued for many years. The main focus has been to regenerate surviving areas and features, including an orchard and the aqueduct. Water systems and ornaments have been repaired, and replanting has been carried out where trees had grown too large, or where plants of the understorey had died out. The combination of lush palm trees and water that characterized many parts of the garden has been successfully revived, and at the same time extensive public access has been built into the plans.

The rich mixture of gardening styles presented by Carmen de los Martires includes a tribute to the city's Moorish legacy in the enclosed Nazarí patio, which has a delicately arched and patterned arcade at one end and a narrow pool in the centre. As the visitor explores the farther reaches of the garden, however, the variety of style becomes apparent. The statue of Neptune rising out of the large circular pool suggests a French influence, while the naturalistic lake and trees fit an English tradition. Secured by municipal ownership and public popularity, the restored gardens represent one of the jewels in the crown of this cultural city.

LEFT
Columnar evergreen cypresses exemplify how the garden's outstanding trees contribute to its quality and interest. It was the felling of many trees in the 1970s that caused alarm and prompted the campaign to save the garden.

Stan Hywet Hall

OHIO • UNITED STATES

When, in 1957, Stan Hywet Hall was donated by the Seiberling family to a nonprofit organization for the benefit of the visiting public, many other fine American estates were facing an uncertain future. Changing fortunes, interests or ownership, and even the ultimate threat of demolition, loomed elsewhere – but not over the Ohio estate of Stan Hywet, created in 1912–15 by Franklin A Seiberling, founder of the Goodyear Tire & Rubber Company, and his wife Gertrude. The gardens were designed chiefly by Boston-based landscape architect Warren Manning and are considered one of the finest examples of his residential work. By the 1950s, however, the gardens had aged and no longer represented the essence of the original design.

The estate encompassed several thousand acres of land in its heyday, of which only 28ha (70 acres) remain. Within this area, trees at the garden's wooded perimeter gradually became overgrown and blocked the vistas that are such an important feature at Stan Hywet. In the formal parts of the garden, mature plants turned sunny borders into shaded spaces, and trees outgrew

their place in the *allées* intended to direct and extend views. Over time, weather ravaged some of the constructed features and the magnificent 1,115 sq m (12,000 sq ft) conservatory collapsed. Then, in the late 1980s, a new period in the garden's history began when a remarkable process of restoration was activated by its state of neglect.

The hall itself was the work of the architect Charles S Schneider, who was influenced by the country houses of the pre-industrial era, such as Compton Wynyates in Warwickshire and Haddon Hall in Derbyshire, that he had seen on a visit to England. His Tudor-revival design for Stan Hywet, while too late to form part of the main Arts and Crafts Movement, was nevertheless inspired by the wish to regain the simpler values of a past age. Other American estates of similar size created in the early twentieth century include the fabulous mansions of Newport, Rhode Island, numerous Long Island edifices, and the European-inspired creations of the industrialist Du Pont family. At Stan Hywet, by contrast, an underlying simplicity of approach is evident, particularly in the gardens.

LEFT
An old photograph
showing an abundance
of iris and peonies
among the flowers in the
cutting garden.

BELOW
Rich yellow rudbeckias
thrive in one of the
revived flower borders.
The replanting of
herbaceous perennials
has been an important
part of continuing
restoration work.

OPPOSITE
Like other industrial
barons of the period,
Franklin A Seiberling
developed an interest in
architecture and poured
some of his wealth into
creating an ideal estate: a
Tudor-revival house set
in gardens notable for
their simplicity of style.

Warren Manning had worked in the office of Frederick Law Olmsted, where large-scale naturalistic landscape designs using native plants played an important part, not only in public projects but also for major residential commissions, including the Biltmore Estate in North Carolina. A commitment to working in partnership with nature was central to Manning's philosophy, and at Stan Hywet he took inspiration from the site's position on a rise above the Cuyahoga River. He wanted the landscape and house to complement one another and so collaborated with Schneider to place the house at an angle from which five distinct dramatic views are possible. With the large doors of the hall thrown open, vistas towards the east and west can be appreciated on a single axis through the house. Manning's design melds formality with a naturalistic approach, and he had a gift for using formal *allées* to extend the garden's main sight-lines towards views over the river valley and to the lagoon that was created out of an old sandstone quarry.

One of these dramatic vistas starts at a long covered porch at the north end of the house, leading for 167m (550ft) along a birch-lined path to views across the valley. The pendulous branches and slanting stems of the birch trees weave magic into the route: patches of light and shade add rhythm, while gaps between the trees allow enticing cross vistas. At the end of the path, a pair of tea-houses afford shelter from which to enjoy the distant landscape or the lush lagoon area closer to hand.

Now restored using birches propagated from the original stock, this vista is as effective today as when first laid out by Manning. In contrast, the rhododendron *allée*, with its upper canopy of London plane trees (*Platanus x hispanica*), awaits full restoration. The trees suffered from being planted in thin topsoil over a layer of rock, but 88 replacements will be replanted in specially prepared root channels. The trees' original positions were located using Manning's specifications and contemporary photographs. Additional rhododendrons, hostas, and shade planting for the understorey will complete the restoration in this area.

The west terrace is one of the masterful achievements of Manning's career. A series of descending lawns combine with other formal elements – a stone terrace, steps, walkways, balustrades, and urns – against a backdrop of mature trees, blending with fine views of rolling hills. Restoration work carried out here in the 1980s has been repeated because mortar mixes acceptable at the time were found to weaken foundations and brickwork, making them susceptible to water damage.

Manning's concept for the walled area later known as the English Garden did not match Gertrude Seiberling's wishes, and in 1929 Manning recommended that she consult

OPPOSITE
An arched doorway into the walled English Garden reveals strong, warm architecture combined with cottage-garden-style planting. This was one of Gertrude Seiberling's favourite places, but its character altered as it became increasingly shaded by trees.

RIGHT
The fine water-goddess fountain sculpted by William Paddock stands in her own small pool and acts as a focal point for the main vista through the English Garden.

renowned landscape architect Ellen Biddle Shipman. Her redesign included a central pool surrounded by borders abundantly planted in cottage-garden style. This became one of Gertrude Seiberling's favourite places, but the neighbouring trees that eventually grew over-large, shading the sun-loving plants beneath, were removed during the 1980s restoration. Shipman's original layout has been retained and is one of the few intact examples of her work open to the public.

The Japanese Garden is currently the focus of structural restoration. Manning planned a miniature landscape using dwarf New England planting stock, but trees added later matured to full size and their weight damaged the cistern that lies beneath the Japanese Garden. The cistern was meant to provide soft rainwater for household use, and although the system proved labour-intensive and was abandoned in the 1930s, it will be renovated to supply water for the garden. The system is linked to the lagoon, which was once a place of recreation for the Seiberlings, complete with changing rooms for swimming. These will be refurbished, as will timber bridges over the water and pathways through the grassy planting on the banks.

ABOVE
As this photograph taken prior to restoration shows, the hedges around the main pool in the English Garden were already larger than planned and obscured the planting behind.

RIGHT
Here is the same scene after restoration, with the hedges cut back to the desired size and wooden planters in the original style replaced at the pool corners.

Stan Hywet Hall has emerged from a period of neglect with the gardens revived by a continuing process of restoration that puts to use expanding knowledge and technology. Sketches and photographs from Manning's archive have been an invaluable aid. The Seiberling family also wisely secured land in the lower valley to preserve fine views in perpetuity. Such attention to detail is important for preserving a design that made as light a mark as possible on an intrinsically beautiful site. While the style of the house and the underlying principles of Manning's approach to landscape design may have been predominantly "English", the results are essentially American.

ABOVE
Vistas are an important feature of the landscape designed by Warren Manning. His birch walk extends for nearly 200m (650ft) from the north end of the house to a viewing point over the Cuyahoga Valley.

Hudson River Gardens

NEW YORK STATE • UNITED STATES

MONTGOMERY PLACE

Montgomery Place is unusual among historic gardens in the United States because it benefited from nearly 200 years of continuous stewardship by members of a single family. The 176ha (434 acre) estate boasts a house in classical-revival style, a fine nineteenth-century landscape with arboretum, beautifully enhanced woodlands, orchards, colourful formal gardens, and impressive natural features and vistas. Its origins are considerably more modest. The land overlooking the Hudson River just outside the town of Annandale was purchased in 1802 as a working farm by Janet Livingston Montgomery, whose family owned a vast estate upriver at Clermont, in the mid-Hudson region.

Janet Montgomery was the wealthy widow of General Richard Montgomery, one of the earliest heroes of the American Revolution; he was killed in the battle for Quebec in 1775. In honour of her late husband, she called her new home Château de Montgomery; its French name was also a reference to her brother's position as Minister to France from 1801 to 1805. Completed in 1805, the mansion commands magnificent westerly views of the Hudson River and Catskill Mountains.

LEFT
An aerial view reveals Montgomery Place's magnificent position beside the Hudson River, with views across to the Catskill Mountains. The site's natural beauty and woodland setting inspired the creation of a fine nineteenth-century landscape.

Against this backdrop, Montgomery developed a commercial nursery and orchards producing apples, pears, and peaches.

Montgomery's immediate heirs died before she did, so in 1828 the estate passed to her younger brother, Edward Livingston, whose working life was spent largely in public service. He and his family used the mansion as a summer home and spent 40 years developing the estate. Alexander Jackson Davis, the architect employed at Lyndhurst and other Hudson Valley estates, was engaged to redesign the house, now called simply Montgomery Place. New wings, porches, and balustrades were added to the building in two phases: the first started in 1842, the second in the early 1860s. Notable surviving architectural features are the classical-style coach house, a Gothic-revival farmhouse, and a Swiss cottage.

The landscape architect Andrew Jackson Downing advised informally on the gardens and grounds. His influence is evident in the curving driveway and elliptical entry court, the stone bridges, and the magnificent groves of trees. He was also involved in creating the woodland walks that wind for 35km (22 miles). This important addition, as well as vistas opened to the river, reveal how seriously Edward Livingston took the responsibility of improving the landscape at Montgomery Place. In 1835, he detailed his gardening activities as: "planting, cutting down, levelling, sloping, opening views, clearing walks, and preparing much work for the ensuing spring to embellish" (correspondence). Edward's daughter, Coralie Barton, designed

some ornamental flower gardens to surround the conservatory.

Even with stability of ownership, the estate faced a period of decline between 1865 and 1921. There was renewed interest in the house and gardens, however, when Montgomery Place passed to General John Ross Delafield. His wife, Violetta, was a talented botanist and keen horticulturist, and the estate flourished until her death in 1949. Her major achievements were to catalogue the flora in the North and South Woods, which she did for her own interest, and to create the series of gardens that stretch from the mansion to the South Woods. These include the area known to the family as the Rough Garden, with rocks and native plants; the contemplative Ellipse Garden; perennial borders; and herb and rose gardens. Another fine achievement was to sculpt the sweeping west lawns and to position a pond here to forge a visual connection with the flowing water of the river beyond.

During the 1950s, Montgomery entered another period of decline, this time lasting almost 40 years. By 1986, when the estate was acquired by the organization now known as Historic Hudson Valley, the property was partially derelict, but restoration was remarkably swift and the estate opened to the public in 1988. Today, Montgomery Place reflects the achievements of the generations of owners who have influenced its

development since 1802. Restoration has been assisted by the considerable amount of written material available. Andrew Jackson Downing's writings proved invaluable, in particular his most important published work, *Landscape Gardening* (1841). Violetta's detailed records, which include diagrams, plant notebooks, journals, plant orders, and invoices, also provided much useful information.

During restoration, the Rough Garden re-emerged from a 1.2m (4ft) covering of nettles with some of its naturalistic planting miraculously intact. The calm enclosure of the minimally planted Ellipse Garden contrasts beautifully with the more densely planted gardens close by. Through an archway, the traditional Herb Garden is once again crisply defined by brick pathways, and its formal borders, radiating out from a central sundial, are cleanly edged. Old-fashioned rose 'Marchesa Boccella', a perpetual, Portland damask type long referred to as the Livingston rose by the family, makes a border around the Rose Garden, where beds of roses are arranged by colour. In acknowledgment of the estate's origins, the orchard has been replanted with fruit varieties grown by Janet Livingston Montgomery. In all, it is hard to disagree with Andrew Jackson Downing's verdict on Montgomery Place, as apt today as when it was written in 1859: "one of our oldest improved country seats

ABOVE
Summer-flowering perennials spill onto a gravel path in the herbaceous borders added by Violetta Delafield, whose interwar schemes have recently been restored. Montgomery Place flourished while in the care of Delafield and her husband.

... nowhere surpassed in America in point of location, natural beauty, or landscape gardening charms" (correspondence).

LYNDHURST

Lyndhurst is a fine edifice set in a superb landscape park in Tarrytown, New York State, enjoying broad views of the Hudson River. The Gothic-revival mansion was built around a smaller-scale villa designed in 1838 by noted architect Alexander Jackson Davis for William Paulding, a former mayor of New York City. Paulding named his imposing villa The Knoll, but critics dubbed it "Paulding's Folly" because of its ecclesiastical lines. It was the first of several estates in the Hudson Valley designed by Davis, who was a friend of the renowned landscape architect Andrew Jackson Downing and was influenced by his ideas on the creation of beautiful landscapes. The garden around Paulding's villa was sculpted into soft, naturalistic areas of lawn punctuated with copses of trees. Picturesque features were created out of naturally occurring

OPPOSITE
The calm Ellipse Garden of Montgomery Place, with its central pool shaded by pine trees, was one of a varied series of features created by Violetta Delafield in 1921–49 and restored with reference to her gardening records.

BELOW
A different view across the Ellipse Garden is captured in this photograph, taken before the most recent period of restoration.

irregularities: rocks became crags, and vistas were expanded by the selective planting and pruning of trees.

Some 25 years later, when Davis was engaged again at Lyndhurst by the new owner, merchant George Merritt, he doubled the size of the building and turned the house into a spectacular mansion. Merritt also hired Ferdinand Mangold, a German horticulturist, to renovate the landscape, and renamed the estate "Lyndenhurst" after the linden trees planted at the time. Mangold was influenced by the ideas of Scottish garden designer and author J C Loudon, who in 1832 invented the term "gardenesque" to describe an aesthetic which differed from the picturesque by placing value on the inherent beauty of a garden and its individual plants, rather than seeking to imitate nature. Mangold's intention was to create well-defined areas of specific interest within the landscape, increasing the range of experience it offered. His plans took time to bear fruit, and many of his ideas were eventually implemented by the next owner, Jay Gould, and his children. Railroads were the source of Gould's wealth, and like other industrialists of the period, he set about using his fortune to create a magnificent estate.

Gould bought "Lyndenhurst", later simplified to Lyndhurst, as a summer estate in 1880 and had elaborate plans for both house and garden. One of his most significant decisions was to rebuild an 1870s conservatory that had burned down. The architect of the new structure, John William Walter, was commissioned to build a superb Gothic-style conservatory to match the house, using a cast-iron frame over the original foundations. When completed, it was the largest private conservatory in America and contained 14 different growing areas for tender plants, including Gould's collection of orchids.

In the gardens, Gould continued the work begun by Mangold by adding hundreds of trees, including copper beeches, sycamores, chestnuts, and maples. The trees were positioned variously to frame views, delineate areas with a

particular atmosphere, or stand as specimens in their own right. A rockery with dark, coniferous planting was made in a forest setting behind the house, combining Downing's picturesque aesthetic with Mangold's gardenesque approach.

In contrast to this expansive nineteenth-century landscape is the intimate rose garden created by Gould's daughter, Helen, who inherited the estate on his death in 1892. It lies near the remains of the grand 1880s conservatory. A Victorian gazebo makes a fine central focal point, with concentric circular beds radiating outwards and arched trellises garlanded in climbing roses. This hub of fragrance displaying a large collection of old-fashioned and modern roses has become one of Lyndhurst's most celebrated features.

After Helen's death in 1938, Lyndhurst passed to her sister, Anna, who maintained the estate until her own death in 1961. Custodianship of the 27ha (67 acres) then passed to the National Trust for Historic Preservation. Today's visitors can follow a specially planted trail to reach nearby Sunnyside, and these two fine gardens will soon be joined by a pathway along the river.

SUNNYSIDE

Washington Irving became one of the United States' first internationally famous writers through short stories such as "The Legend of Sleepy Hollow" and "Rip Van Winkle", both published in 1819–20. He was born in New York City in 1783, the youngest child of Scottish immigrants, and was named after the great hero of the American Revolution (and future first president of the United States), George Washington. After training as a lawyer, Irving spent the years 1815 to 1832 living and writing in Europe, during which time he served in the American diplomatic corps in London. Spain held a particular fascination for Irving, and while living there he wrote *The Life and Times of Christopher Columbus* (1828), the first English-language biography of the explorer, and *The Alhambra* (1832), a

ABOVE
Lyndhurst became renowned for its circular Rose Garden centred around a domed Victorian gazebo. This was an addition made by Jay Gould's daughter, Helen, who inherited the estate in 1892.

ABOVE
Lyndhurst's ruined 1870s conservatory was rebuilt in Gothic style by Jay Gould and was the largest in America when completed.

RIGHT
Arched trellises punctuate the Rose Garden at Lyndhurst, and support climbing roses that add to the mass of bloom and fragrance. This romantic scene contrasts with the surrounding landscape of softly sculpted lawn and copses.

ABOVE
Washington Irving
settled at Sunnyside after
many years in Europe.
He adapted the modest
cottage to reflect his own
taste, and the front door
is still romantically
enveloped by the
wisteria he planted.

series of sketches based on the Moorish fortified palace in Granada. Towards the end of his life, Irving wrote a five-volume biography of George Washington, whom he reputedly met as a young child. He considered it his greatest work and it remained the definitive version for many years.

When Irving returned to settle in America after 17 years in Europe, he moved into a house in a beautiful part of the Hudson Valley that was to become liberally sprinkled with great estates and summer retreats. The property was a small Dutch-style farmhouse close to the Hudson River in Tarrytown, New York State. With the help of his neighbour, the artist George Harvey, Irving set about turning the eighteenth-century stone cottage into the quirky retreat named Sunnyside (but popularly known as "Sleepy Hollow"). Irving wrote: "It is a beautiful spot capable of being made a little paradise" (correspondence). The perfect place for him to put down some roots.

His life and travels were reflected in the architectural features he added to the cottage. The Dutch stepped gables and weathervanes were reminders of colonial New York buildings he had observed during childhood; Sunnyside's turrets and rooflines echoed buildings he came to know in Scotland and Spain. Having established his retreat, Irving was lured back to Spain in 1842, where he served for four years as envoy to the court of Queen Isabella II. On his return, he made the house more spacious with the addition of a tower that became known to his friends as the "pagoda", even though Spanish monasteries were the major design influence.

Irving was a romantic, which shaped his view of nature, art, and history. It also naturally informed the way he designed his garden to sit harmoniously within the magnificent surroundings. Rolling lawns extended up to the house and down towards the river. Colourful flowers were combined with vegetables and herbs in a lushly planted kitchen garden. A stone-banked pond was created and named his "Little Mediterranean". All these features, and a stream fringed with meadow wild flowers, fit seamlessly into the bucolic landscape. Against the house Irving planted a wisteria, which, when

OPPOSITE, ABOVE
Woven wooden
pyramids in this
flower-filled corner
of the kitchen garden
emphasize the level
of detail to which the
original features have
been restored. Memoirs
written by Irving's many
visitors were a rich
source of information.

OPPOSITE, BELOW
Where fruit trees in
a sweep of lawn once
again blend with the
natural surroundings,
the memorable vista
over the nearby
Hudson River has
now been opened up.

draping the cottage with flowers, adds a distinctly fairy-tale quality to the setting.

In spite of being a lifelong bachelor, Irving did not lead a solitary existence. His home was peopled with visiting friends and family, many of whose written and pictorial impressions of Sunnyside proved an invaluable resource when it came to restoring the house and landscape. After Irving's death in 1859, Sunnyside remained the home of his family and descendants until 1945, when it was acquired by a preservation body set up by the great philanthropist, antiquarian, and crusading preservationist, John D Rockefeller Jr. With his own home, Kykuit, located close by, Rockefeller was extremely interested in the history of "Sleepy Hollow". Sunnyside was opened to the public in 1947, making it one of the first mid-nineteenth-century houses established as a house museum, a landmark in American architectural preservation.

In the 1950s, influenced by the restoration practices at Williamsburg in Virginia (see page 196), a decision was made to return the house and garden at Sunnyside to how they looked during Irving's lifetime. This meant removing a wing added to the rear of the house in 1896, as well as reconstructing lost areas, including the unusual ice house and the fenced-in kitchen yard. Sunnyside's survival was ensured by its architectural merit, but even more decisive was its association with a national icon. Its restoration is a tribute to the man who was an ambassador in the broadest sense, a conduit for American and European culture.

DESIGNERS & PLANTSMEN

Certain gardens are restored because they were created, either entirely or in part, by someone who is widely admired for their achievements in a particular field, whether in literature, politics, or science. The same is true for gardens shaped by the major players in garden history, interest in whom has grown enormously since the mid-twentieth century. The will to perpetuate the gardens or planting schemes of such influential figures as Gertrude Jekyll is particularly strong because the physical evidence of their work is so vulnerable to change and loss.

Upton Grey

HAMPSHIRE · ENGLAND

When Rosamund and John Wallinger became the new owners of the Manor House at Upton Grey in 1983, they had no idea of its connection with Gertrude Jekyll. They had no inkling, either, that they would devote more than 10 years to restoring the planting schemes Jekyll designed for the garden here. In those early days, when they were busy making the neglected house habitable again, Ros Wallinger admits that she had little notion of Jekyll's importance to British garden history: "I knew that she was a nineteenth-century Surrey gardener, that her gardening boots had become almost as famous as their owner. I knew very little else about her" (Wallinger, 2000: 16). During the next few years, however, she was to become a great deal more knowledgeable about the woman who had such a widespread influence on British gardening in the twentieth century.

Born in London in 1843, Jekyll was trained as an artist and began designing gardens at the age of 36. Her style combined meticulous attention to detail with intricate, and often adventurous, plantsmanship. She undertook some 400 commissions in all, famously working in partnership with the young architect Edwin Lutyens from the mid-1890s. In spite of Jekyll's high reputation during her lifetime, none of her major gardens have survived intact, and very few features remain in the gardens where she contributed planting schemes. It is fortunate that her precisely articulated ideas and sentiments are

RIGHT
Research into the history of the house soon led on to the discovery that Gertrude Jekyll had designed the gardens in c.1908. This photograph of her was taken at Upton Grey.

OPPOSITE
Laid out on one of the upper terraces behind the Arts and Crafts house, the restored Rose Lawn demonstrates the combination of harmonious planting and well-planned structure at which Jekyll excelled.

preserved in gardening books such as *Wood & Garden* (1899), *Roses for English Gardens* (1902), and *Colour in the Flower Garden* (1908). Her views on colour and planting in drifts, on the use of plants to complement architectural features, and on the value of particular groups of plants, such as English natives, reached a wide audience.

For the Wallingers, it was the knowledge that "very few other Jekyll gardens were complete or fully restorable that spurred our determination to make Upton Grey as accurate a living museum as possible" (Wallinger, 2000: 29). They chose to embark on an authentic restoration of the derelict garden, rather than the more modest option of rejuvenation and replanting. The journey that lead to this decision began in spring 1984, when research into the Grade II listed house, located near Basingstoke in Hampshire, revealed its importance to the Arts and Crafts Movement. It was designed around the shell of an earlier Tudor farmhouse by the architect Ernest Newton, for a wealthy businessman, Charles Holme, who in 1893 founded an influential journal entitled *The Studio*. Making use of surviving plans, the Wallingers restored the house accurately to Newton's design.

For the garden, the library of the Royal Institute of British Architects in London held the first clue. The Wallingers found a note among Ernest Newton's papers that read: "Garden, possibly by Gertrude Jekyll" (quoted in Wallinger, 2000: 16). They next contacted landscape historian and Jekyll specialist Richard Bisgrove at the University of Reading, who pointed them towards the archive of Jekyll designs and planting plans held in the Reef Point Gardens Collection at the University of California at Berkeley. Enquiries there lead to a breakthrough: they had found Jekyll's detailed plans for 19 borders at Upton Grey. Once Ros Wallinger had taken delivery of copies, however, she realized that these were working documents rather than the finished versions that Jekyll presented to her clients. The handwriting was hard to decipher, peppered with abbreviations, and the plant names were written in dense clusters.

Among the papers that arrived from Berkeley were two architectural plans dated 1908, drawn up by the Basingstoke firm that carried out the building work to Newton's design. These showed how the 2ha (5 acre) garden was laid out on two sides of the long house, with a formal garden in a series of

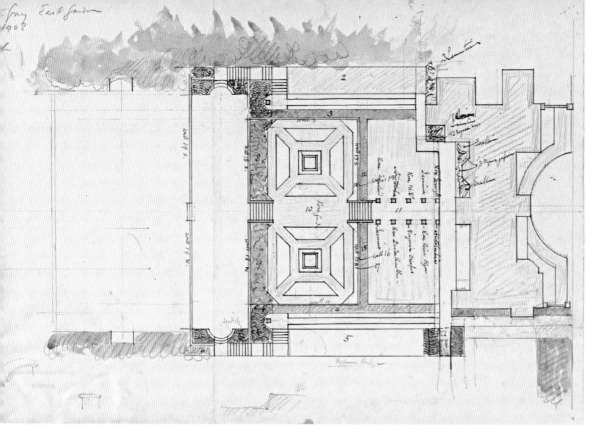

LEFT
Jekyll's original plans for the garden, held in an archive in California, were used as the basis of a minutely detailed restoration by the Wallingers, owners of Upton Grey since 1983. This plan of the West Garden shows a series of formal terraces descending from the house on the right.

BELOW
The West Garden today, as viewed from an upper window of the house, provides an accurate picture of Jekyll's style.

OPPOSITE
Before replanting could begin on the Rose Lawn, the long-vanished pattern of beds and fine turf had to be reinstated. Eryngiums and other long-lasting perennials were chosen by Jekyll to compensate for the short flowering season of the roses.

terraces at the back and a wild garden in front. Armed with the necessary evidence, and with the support of garden designer and historian Penelope Hobhouse, as well as the Hampshire Gardens Trust, the Wallingers were able to progress from the clearance of brambles and other weeds to a full-scale restoration. The initial work involved structural repairs, especially to the retaining walls of the terraces (built of Bargate sandstone, which Jekyll used in her own garden at Munstead Wood, Surrey) and to the flights of steps leading between levels. The garden's original layout was obscured by the dilapidated state of these features, the undergrowth smothering once-immaculate lawns, and the mature trees, including an enormous beech and two towering conifers, that had either been added later or were self-sown.

The formal terraced garden slowly re-emerged as work continued in the summer of 1984. The pergola by the house,

essential to the central vista on the upper level, was rebuilt, with thick rope hung between oak posts and draped in climbers such as rambling roses "The Garland" and "Blush Rambler". From the end of the pergola, stone steps lead down between retaining walls to the rose lawn, where the pattern of beds was reinstated. From here, central steps lead down to a long, rectangular lawn called the bowling green; finally, beyond a low bank, lies the tennis court lawn. On the far side of this, a rose arbour marks the central view back across the garden towards the house. On the upper two terraces are a series of herbaceous borders that were planned by Jekyll to reach their peak together in summer, and yet each to be individual in their appearance.

For the wild garden on the other side of the house, Jekyll's plan was for mown grass paths to wind through longer grass planted with bulbs and wild flowers, with focal points

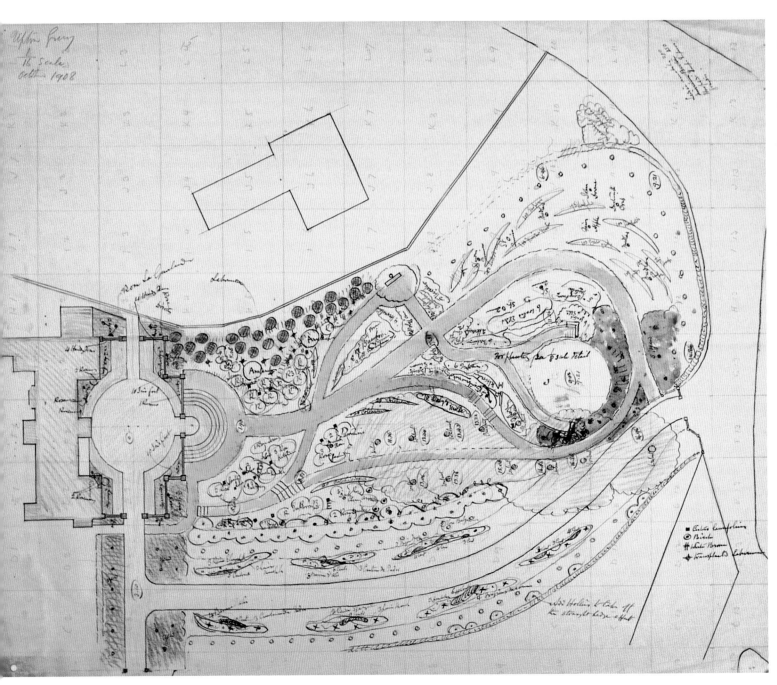

ABOVE
A hedge screens the
ebulliently planted
kitchen garden, keeping
it separate from the
terraces overlooked
from the house.

OPPOSITE
Jekyll was an advocate
of wild gardens and
designed one at Upton
Grey to contrast with the
formal terraces on the
other side of the house.
Her plan for the East
Garden shows winding
paths leading from
semicircular steps to
a round pond.

provided by a circular pond and carefully associated groups of trees and shrubs. The Wallinger's early clearance work revealed some of the daffodil varieties planted by Jekyll in curving drifts. These were retained, but a group of Japanese cherries and other later additions unsympathetic to Jekyll's design were removed, as were rogue trees and shrubs. Beyond the wrought-iron gates marking the entrance to the wild garden, the semicircle of shallow grass steps was uncovered and rebuilt, completing the subtle progression out from the house's forecourt. Later, after the pond was cleared and refilled, replanting began. Groups of roses such as *R. arvensis* and rambling "Jersey Beauty" were an important element; walnuts were added to the nuttery, and leading to the pond were kniphofias, tree lupins, and iris.

Tracking down the plants chosen by Jekyll was a vital element of the restoration, but it often proved to be a daunting task. Many cultivars had become rare and some, it seemed, had even disappeared. Ros Wallinger had despaired of finding pink-flowered rose "Madame Caroline Testout", a hybrid tea type that Jekyll used in the rose lawn, when she came across it quite

by chance in 1988 during a visit to the Roseraie de l'Haÿ-les-Roses, near Paris. Most of Jekyll's plants were eventually located and used to recreate combinations such as rich pink *Paeonia lactiflora* "Sarah Bernhardt" with old shrub roses and royal lilies (*Lilium regale*) for the beds of the rose lawn; or the different pinks (dianthus), dwarf phlox, and sedums that sprout, as if naturally, from the drystone walls; or indeed the old-fashioned aquilegias, rudbeckias, and helianthus among the array of plants in the herbaceous borders.

Some two decades after work began, the restored garden at Upton Grey has achieved its own sense of maturity. The garden is remarkable as an accurate representation of Jekyll's style and is astonishing for its depth of detail. Few owners of "lost" gardens created by Jekyll are able to restore them to her original designs, even where sufficient evidence has survived, because of other obstacles. Sections of land have often been sold for development, or swimming pools and hard tennis courts stand in the way. Some owners "simply do not want to restore their adequate gardens to labour-intensive Jekyll originals" (Wallinger, 2000: 29). The Wallingers, however, are glad to have followed in Jekyll's footsteps, and continue to be inspired by her formidable talent and uncompromising standards.

ABOVE
Lead cherubs flank the gates into the East Garden, where clearance of overgrown vegetation revealed some of the daffodils originally planted by Jekyll. This area rich in bulbs and wild flowers is a delight in spring.

RIGHT
Rosamund Wallinger describes the garden as a reproduction of Jekyll's art. She found that while some of the herbaceous plants in Jekyll's plans are still popular today, others have become rare, and these took several years to trace.

RIGHT
Lush-leaved bergenia
and pink peonies were
both firm favourites
with Jekyll. The effortless
beauty of this replanted
border gives no hint of
the commitment needed
to maintain it.

The Mount

MASSACHUSETTS • USA

The house and garden of novelist Edith Wharton, in Lenox, western Massachusetts, survived several changes of ownership and a period of neglect to become, by 2003, a national monument to her achievements as a writer and designer. Best known for works such as *The House of Mirth* (1905) and *Ethan Frome* (1911), Wharton wrote more than 40 books in as many years and, for *The Age of Innocence* (1920), was the first woman to receive the Pulitzer Prize for fiction. Her success at writing provided a means to break free from the social constrictions of the New York high society into which she was born in 1862.

In addition to fiction, Wharton wrote books and essays on architecture, gardens, interior design, and travel. *The Decoration of Houses* (1897), which she wrote with the architect Ogden Codman, proved highly influential. The book advocated open, light-filled rooms to replace the stuffy Victorian-style interiors that prevailed. Wharton also influenced contemporary taste in gardens through her authoritative *Italian Villas and their Gardens* (1904), published while she was living at The Mount. This was the place where she put her ideas into practice, as the designer of both the white stucco house, in classical-revival style, and the 1.2ha (3 acres) of formal gardens.

OPPOSITE
Edith Wharton wrote an influential book about the gardens of Italy, which she had learned about during travels in Europe, and put her knowledge into practice when she designed her own Italianate sunken garden in the early 1900s.

BELOW
The well-proportioned main vista that runs parallel to the house, now restored, demonstrates Edith Wharton's firmly held belief that garden design should be treated as an extension of architecture.

It was in 1901, when Wharton was almost 40, that she and her husband Teddy purchased 46ha (113 acres) of farmland in the Berkshire Hills on which to build what she described as her first real home. The house, positioned on a rise to enjoy a panoramic view of the surrounding hills and lakes, was completed in 1902. Here the Whartons lived for almost 10 years; it was a productive time for Edith Wharton as a writer, but not a long period in garden-making terms. She described her daily routine at The Mount in a letter to a friend: "Here I write every morning, and then devote myself to horticulture; while Teddy plays golf and cuts down trees" (correspondence).

Her writing room opened onto a wide, paved terrace, with views across two grass terraces leading down to the Lime Walk, an *allée* planted with linden trees. A rectangular flower garden, 30m by 33m (100ft by 110ft) in size and filled with annuals and perennials in bright shades, is linked by the axis of the Lime Walk to an Italianate sunken garden enclosed by 3m (10ft) stone walls and hedges. The four large quadrants of grass laid out within this 24m (80ft) square surround a circular fountain with a rocky base, and the planting is predominantly of white flowers. The walls are pierced by arches framing fabulous views, and a stone pergola clad in a grapevine marks the entrance to a meadow that becomes vibrant with daisies in high season.

Even though Wharton was confident enough about her own ideas to produce the preliminary layout for the main gardens and orchards, she also consulted her niece, Beatrix Jones (later Farrand), who was a founding member of the American Society of Landscape Architects. Farrand designed the 0.8km (half-mile) approach to The Mount, which sweeps through the hilly landscape, passing an *allée* of sugar maples and crossing a brook before arriving at the house's gravelled forecourt. She chose to leave working areas of the estate exposed to view, in contrast to the English Landscape tradition, still in vogue, which favoured using decorative facades to conceal such mundane features as stables, sheds, and kitchen gardens.

Wharton was pleased with the garden, as she acknowledged in a letter to her close friend, Morton Fullerton: "I am amazed at the success of my efforts. Decidedly, I'm a better landscape gardener than novelist, and this place, every line of which is my own work, far surpasses *The House of Mirth*" (correspondence). In 1911, however, the Whartons sold The Mount and their marriage of 26 years came to an end. Edith Wharton moved permanently to France, where she continued to write and make gardens. She was also involved in war relief work during World War I, and was made a Knight of the French Legion of Honour. She died in 1937 and is buried in Versailles.

The Lenox estate where she had lived so contentedly remained a private residence until 1942, when it became part of the neighbouring Foxhollow School for Girls. The grounds were generally well maintained during the school's period of ownership, and in 1976 the last headmistress had the foresight to nominate The Mount to the National Register of Historic Places. In spite of this attempt to secure its future, The Mount was sold to a developer in 1977 and then to a theatre group the

Wharton's close involvement with The Mount sets it apart from other American estates of the same era, many created with a much larger budget than was at her disposal. Her understanding of architecture was gained largely through self-education and extensive travels in Europe. As is clear from the restored gardens at The Mount, Wharton was immersed in European gardening traditions and admired the great Renaissance gardens of Italy. She considered that a garden should be an architectural composition, divided into "rooms", and designed both as a complementary extension to the house and in sympathy with the natural landscape. It was also important to her that a garden should possess "a charm independent of the seasons" (correspondence).

During a visit to England in the late 1890s, she met author and plantswoman Gertrude Jekyll, and found her approach to planting of great interest. The idea of doing away with annual bedding planted around greenhouse exotics chimed with Wharton's desire to extend her own fresh approach to interior design into the garden. Ample borders stuffed with exuberant displays of perennials allowed for great freedom of expression within a simple but formal framework of walls, steps, terraces, and paths.

OPPOSITE
Edith Wharton was a
passionate gardener, and
her very personal garden
at The Mount provided
a setting conducive
to writing and
entertaining friends.

BELOW
The dolphin fountain in
the flower garden aligns
with the main vista. In
the background is an
avenue of young lime
trees; these replace the
originals that had
vanished by the 1980s.

BELOW
Years of painstaking
work have revived
The Mount's classical
elegance, both indoors
and out. The design of
the main house was
inspired by an English
country house built in
Palladian style in the
seventeenth-century.

year after. By the early 1980s, the garden had lost some of its key features. The terraces descending from the house were still outlined in hedges of arbor-vitae (*Thuja occidentalis*), but these had become over-mature thickets. Bushes and clipped topiary shapes had also grown huge. The Lime Walk and most other paths had disappeared under a tide of grass. The formal pools were cracked, and the dolphin fountain from the Flower Garden had been moved to the sunken Walled Garden.

Plans to save the house and garden were laid in the 1980s, although they did not reach fruition until a large grant was secured in 1999. The first step was taken by the National Trust for Historic Preservation, which helped found a nonprofit organization named Edith Wharton Restoration (EWR) to protect and manage The Mount. But there was an inherent conflict of interests between the resident theatre group and the

The Mount — Residence of Mr. E. R. Wharton, Lenox, Mass.

LEFT
A similar view of the house and garden in its heyday is shown in this old postcard. On the slope beside the house can be seen the grey boulders of the rockery where Wharton planted native ferns.

preservationists of the EWR, which, compounded by financial difficulties, meant that the approach to restoration remained piecemeal. Nevertheless, in 1982 Harvard University's Graduate School of Design carried out a study of the grounds, and, with limited structural work, the building and gardens survived the decade.

With the committed efforts of the EWR, a comprehensive programme of restoration finally began in 1992 and was boosted in 1999 by funds from Save America's Treasures (SAT), a federal programme supporting preservation projects nationwide. It announced a grant of almost $3 million (£1.52 million) to match the funds already raised by EWR. Just under half of the total budget was earmarked for landscape restoration, which was headed by Susan Child, a Boston-based landscape architect. Few of Wharton's plans for The Mount have survived, but Farrand's archive, held at the University of California at Berkeley, proved invaluable in reconstructing the garden.

Child and her team were also guided by an abundance of written material, including Wharton's letters to friends such as fellow-novelist Henry James, in addition to contemporary photographs; archaeological digs revealed the dimensions of the paths and materials used. The replanting, however, required some compromises: the Walled Garden, once filled with sun-loving plants but now shaded by trees, has been planted with alternatives that can thrive without full sun. Similarly, box

(*Buxus sempervirens*) has been used to replace hedges of hemlock (*Tsuga*), a conifer susceptible to sap-sucking insects called adelgids.

While much work to the garden has been completed, some projects remain on hold. The kitchen garden designed by Farrand, for example, would take an estimated $1 million (£503,900) to restore. Even so, the house and grounds shine anew with Edith Wharton's creative talents, embodying her tastes and character, and illustrating her way of life. The Mount honours a celebrated novelist who was also a passionate gardener.

ABOVE
The reconstructed stone pergola, clothed in vines as Wharton intended, exemplifies the architectural strength of the garden. It leads from the Italian garden into a meadow that blends with the surrounding countryside.

OPPOSITE
Curving gently towards the house, this tree-lined drive was the main contribution made by Wharton's niece, landscape gardener Beatrix Farrand. The scene in autumn reveals the romantic side of The Mount.

Villa la Pietra

FLORENCE • ITALY

The gardens of Villa La Pietra, on the outskirts of Florence, have been restored twice. The first restoration was undertaken in the early twentieth century by Arthur Acton, an English aesthete and art collector. He recreated a Renaissance garden around the fifteenth-century villa at the heart of the 23ha (57-acre) estate, thus providing an elegant setting for his distinguished collection of Italian statues. The garden was at its zenith in the 1930s, but by the 1990s much of the planting was in need of rejuvenation – prompting the second restoration. This has recently been completed by New York University, which now owns the estate, and the garden has been returned as accurately as possible to Acton's design.

Born in London to an English-Italian family, Acton showed an early interest in fine art. He worked for a number of years as interior decorator for the fashionable American architect Stanford White, and in 1903 married Hortense Mitchell, the daughter of a wealthy, cultivated businessman from Chicago. Acton and his wife spent their lives acquiring, restoring, and furnishing a number of historic villas around Florence.

ABOVE
The golden stone of the villa merges harmoniously with evergreen stone pines and cypresses.

OPPOSITE
The garden's central vista leads to a panorama across the city of Florence. Until the recent restoration was carried out, this was one of the views obscured by dense plant growth.

ABOVE
The open-air theatre has
been restored to Arthur
Acton's concept. It is a
composition of statues,
balustrades, and
evergreen topiary in
which the stage is a
stretch of lawn and
clipped box plants
represent the footlights.

RIGHT
A photograph of the
theatre taken in the
1930s captures it when
still in its well-controlled
youth. The pattern of
sunlight and shade on
grass was an important
element throughout this
essentially green garden

OPPOSITE
Sir Harold Acton,
pictured here in a grotto
at Villa La Pietra, was
passionate about the
garden made by his
father and ensured its
continued preservation
after his lifetime by
leaving the estate to
the care of New
York University.

Villa La Pietra was owned by a succession of leading Florentine families after its completion in 1462, and the terraced garden originally created here by Francesco Sassetti, financier to the Medici family, is recorded in a drawing by Giorgio Vasari the younger (held in Florence's Uffizi gallery). The villa was sold in the 1540s to the Capponi family, after which the building was considerably altered. Cardinal Capponi added the baroque facade that greets visitors today and his family crest still adorns the entrance gateway. During the nineteenth century, Capponi's descendants replaced the formal Italian garden with a landscape park in the English style: a *giardino inglese*.

The Actons bought Villa La Pietra in 1902, at a time when Anglo-American admiration for Italian Renaissance gardens and architecture was at its height. Arthur Acton expressly set about creating an English interpretation of an Italian garden, as recalled by his son, the scholar and writer Harold Acton, in *Memoirs of an Aesthete* (first published in 1948):

> The original garden, laid out on a steep hill-side, was almost destroyed in the nineteenth century when so-called "English gardens" were all the rage, and it is ironical that my father, an Englishman, should have restored and reconstructed on pure Tuscan lines. The process of "tuscanization" began just before my birth, and my father refined upon the traces of the former garden and its retaining walls, with all the creative ingenuity of a *cinquecento* architect. (Acton, 1970: 7)

The concept of the garden was essentially Acton's, but he took some initial advice from the French landscape architect Achille Duchêne, who was well-known for his recreations of classical gardens. The main work to the garden at Villa La Pietra was carried out in 1908–10, with further restoration undertaken in 1915 by Diego Suarez, the Colombian-born landscape architect who trained under Acton and went on to design the Italianate gardens of Vizcaya, Florida, in the 1920s.

The approach to Villa La Pietra along a straight avenue of tall cypress trees sets a suitably theatrical tone for the main garden, which is laid out on terraces on one side of the house. Acton's principle aim was to create a series of enclosures linked by flights of steps and paths, and to fill them with Italian statues dating mainly from the seventeenth and eighteenth centuries. His greatest accomplishment is the three-way harmony between the terraced enclosures, the clipped yew and box hedges, and the classical statues. The overriding feeling is one of discovery, as grass or gravel paths lead beneath evergreen holm oaks and stone pines to marble figures, urns, a curving Corinthian colonnade, and stone fountains.

Sir Harold Acton described the garden as "essentially green; other colours are episodic and incidental. Sunlight and shade are as carefully distributed as the fountains, terraces and statues, and in no other private Florentine garden have I seen statues of such individual strength and grace". (Acton, 1970: 11) The single most notable statue is the figure of Hercules by the Renaissance sculptor Orazio Marinali, whose work Acton acquired wherever

possible. Classical figures by Francesco Bonazza grace the stage of the garden's memorable green theatre, where clipped balls of green box represent footlights and yew hedges form the wings; and the broad terrace that runs along the villa's garden front, providing a dramatic view over the lower terraces, is bounded by statues standing on a stone balustrade.

Since little trace remained of how the grounds had looked before being landscaped in the nineteenth century, Acton largely followed his own ideal of a sixteenth-century garden. On the north side of the house, however, an historically significant feature had survived, in the form of a seventeenth-century *pomario*, or walled orchard. It was enclosed by baroque walls surmounted by alternating busts and finials, and richly decorated with artificial rockwork in a manner termed *rocaille*. Acton repaired the paths, and he introduced lemon and orange trees in great terracotta pots in reference to the original use of the *pomario*. A glasshouse at one end of the orchard served as their winter quarters. The restoration Acton carried out here, before tackling the main garden, inspired much of the later work.

Sir Harold inherited Villa La Pietra following his father's death in 1953, and he faithfully preserved the garden that he

OPPOSITE
Arthur Acton chose the
statues for his garden
with meticulous care
and in the process built
up an outstanding
collection of
seventeenth- and
eighteenth-century
Italian figures.

RIGHT
Renaissance-inspired
classical symmetry
characterizes the
garden's central vista,
with the fifteenth-
century villa in the
background. At its height
in the 1920s–30s, Villa La
Pietra was considered
one of Italy's most
beautiful gardens.

had been brought up to admire with passion. Although he made few changes, the framework of trees, hedges, and topiary specimens gradually grew well beyond their intended size and, in the process, obscured the garden's original design and blocked essential vistas. Sir Harold died in 1994, having secured the future of Villa La Pietra and his father's significant art collection by bequeathing the estate to New York University to be used as a centre for academic study. The university has overseen the sensitive revival of Arthur Acton's garden by the distinguished English landscape architect Kim Wilkie, who trained at the University of California at Berkeley, and has an international practice specializing in historic garden restoration.

The main task has been to rejuvenate the structural planting. Old trees in the garden and olive groves in the surrounding estate were replanted with young stock and, where necessary, evergreen hedges were cut back to an appropriate size. As a result, the different spaces within the garden have regained their proper proportions in the best Renaissance tradition, restoring a sense of balance to the whole composition. Equally important, Acton's tree-framed views have been re-opened to reveal the surrounding hills and, in one direction, Florence and its cathedral. The statues have been cleaned and the complex water system has also been modernized.

Wilkie's work as a landscape architect has always focused on the relationship between people and landscape, perpetuating the humanist tradition of the early Italian Renaissance that had also inspired Arthur Acton. In the case of Villa La Pietra, Wilkie gently resuscitated the established, complex garden, without creating an unwelcome veneer of novelty. While respecting the qualities of the site, he successfully restored the balance of its form and contents, both architectural and horticultural, and the garden today presents the Renaissance image so cherished by Acton.

ABOVE
The seventeenth-
century walled *pomario*
shelters lemon and
orange trees in large
terracotta pots. It was
the only early feature
to have survived when
the gardens were
landscaped in the
nineteenth century.

East Lambrook Manor

SOMERSET · ENGLAND

In 1936 Margery Fish was 43 years old, living in London, and working as a journalist on the *Daily Mail*. At that point in her life she would have seemed an unlikely person soon to make a lasting impression as a plantswoman, gardener, and author, but a decision to move to the country in 1937 resulted in a remarkable change of direction. She and her husband, Walter, bought East Lambrook Manor, located near South Petherton in Somerset, where they faced "a poor battered old house that had to be gutted to be liveable, and a wilderness instead of a garden" (Fish, 1995: 12).

Their friends thought the couple would enjoy renovating the house but wondered how they would ever tame the wilderness. However, not only did they succeed in making an outstanding garden, Margery Fish endeared herself to an audience of thousands by sharing her experiences through numerous magazine articles and the seven books she wrote between 1956 and 1966. In summing up Fish's achievements at East Lambrook Manor in the context of British horticulture, former head of gardens to the National Trust John Sales has

LEFT
The garden is intimately connected to the manor house, around which it revolves in perfect partnership. The scene in 1937 was very different, when Margery Fish and her husband bought a battered house surrounded by a farmyard.

commented: "In the development of gardening in the second half of the twentieth century no garden has yet had a greater effect and no garden writer has had a more profound influence." (Sales, 1980: 149)

After her husband's death in 1949, Margery Fish continued developing the garden on her own for another 20 years. By the time of her own death in 1969, East Lambrook Manor had become a place of pilgrimage for garden enthusiasts. It struck a popular chord in a way few other well-known gardens of the time were able to, largely because the informal style Fish advocated could easily be adapted to the needs of the growing number of weekend and novice gardeners with small-scale gardens.

The manor house was built of local Ham stone, and, although large, it was not a grand building and thus lent itself to the cottage-garden approach that Margery Fish set out to explore. When she and her husband initially planned the garden, they provided it with a structure of paths and low walls, and an arrangement of lawns, trees, and hedges. But it was not Margery Fish's intention to create an architectural garden; the structure provided a framework for planting, and this is where her true talent lay. Her increasing knowledge of

ABOVE
In this sunny corner of the garden, vertical spires of flowers and foliage punctuate the mass of low-growing perennials, which were planted densely to keep weeds at bay.

RIGHT
Evergreen foliage plants, such as the grey-leaved artemisias in this silver-and-white border, provide colour and form throughout the year at East Lambrook Manor. Margery Fish advised her readers that a garden should be pleasant and interesting in all seasons.

old-fashioned varieties of perennials, bulbs, and small shrubs enabled her to develop a brilliant array of plant associations in which size, shape, foliage, and season of interest were as important as flower colour.

The garden was less than 0.8ha (2 acres) in size but its terrain offered varied growing conditions, and these Margery Fish turned to her advantage. In the hot, south-facing area by the house, she made a paved garden filled with low-growing pinks (dianthus), thymes, mints, and other heat-loving gems, such as the disregarded, daisy-flowered *Erigeron karvinskianus* (also known as *E. mucronatus*) and *Campanula carpatica*. Along the marshy banks of a ditch that ran through the garden, she spread tiny violets and primroses. An ancient malt-house became the support for climbers and wall plants such as *Ceanothus x veitchianus*, clematis "Ville de Lyon", and *Chimonanthus praecox*. The main lawn was planted with maples, cherries, willows, and other favourite trees. A contrast to the densely planted borders that reigned at East Lambrook Manor was provided by a path lined simply with the grey-green conifer *Chamaecyparis lawsoniana* "Fletcheri", which Fish clipped into neat domes.

The garden became known for the richness of its plant collections, but it was the way in which Fish combined plants that was particularly instructive for her growing audience. She planted assemblies of perennials closely together in order to smother weeds, which was something of a novel idea in the 1950s. She also favoured planting for year-round enjoyment in preference to a zenith of summer flowers, and used shapely evergreen foliage plants such as euphorbias and bergenias to help clothe the garden in all seasons. It was one of her guiding principles that "a good garden is the garden you enjoy looking at even in the depths of winter". (Fish, 1995: 14)

Fish's readers found her down-to-earth advice appealing and enjoyed the many stories associated with her. She recommended "plentiful libations of washing-up water and mulchings with tea leaves" for healthy primroses and told of how, during World War II, she willingly exchanged her precious ration of tea for a rare variety of double primrose (Fish, 1995: 146). The secret of her popular appeal was perhaps in the simplicity of her suggestions and the homely, conversational tone of the articles she wrote for *Amateur Gardening* and *The Field*. In *We Made a Garden*, first published in 1956, she confessed: "Of course we have made mistakes, endless mistakes, but at least they were our own, just as the garden was our own. However imperfect the result, there is a certain satisfaction in making a garden that is like no one else's, and in knowing that you yourself are responsible for every stone and every flower in the place." (Fish, 1995: 12)

OPPOSITE
The garden's wealth of plants today recalls the high reputation it held in the 1960s, when it was home to some 2000 different types of plant.

ABOVE
Areas where plants mesh together in colonies look wilder than formal borders, but soon lose their poise without the close attention of a gardener. Sensitive intervention was needed in the 1980s to curb vigorous plants.

Fish was widely admired for making such a personal garden, created and maintained with little outside help. She knew every plant in the garden and wrote of them with affection: "In course of time they become real friends, conjuring up pleasant associations of the people who gave them and the gardens they came from." (Fish, 1995: 13) By the 1960s, the garden contained an estimated 2,000 different plant species and cultivars, including unusual forms of English natives, and many of these were made more widely available through a small nursery attached to the garden. Fish's praise of old varieties that had fallen out of favour created a revival of interest among gardeners across Britain.

It was always bound to be a daunting challenge to nurture the garden after Fish's death, not least because so many of the plants were unusual, unlabelled and known only to her. East Lambrook Manor was initially inherited by members of her family, who looked after the garden courageously; but by the early 1980s there were signs of gentle decline. More serious was the possibility that the sale of the house could bring an end to this important and tangible part of her gardening legacy. The local district council deemed the garden sufficiently important to impose preservation orders on all the trees and shrubs until the new owners were able to outline their plans for the garden.

East Lambrook Manor was very fortunately bought by Andrew Norton, who had a natural affinity for the place because his mother had been a keen gardener and a great admirer of Margery Fish. While accepting that a personal garden of this sort could never be recreated exactly, he decided to re-establish the garden's overall form and the character of its individual plant colonies. He was extremely fortunate in finding that Fish's former part-time gardener, Maureen Whitty, was still living in the village. She was able to shed light on what plants grew in different areas, particularly where rarities had died out or been smothered by stronger-growing plants. Norton was also able to establish a national collection of hardy geraniums (cranesbills) at East Lambrook, to champion a perennial that Fish valued very highly.

By the time that Norton sold the house and its garden to its present owners, work was well under way, and this work has been continued with much enthusiasm by Robin and Marianne Williams. They have embarked upon a programme of careful restoration, taking each area of the garden in turn so as to reinforce the overall structure. They are also carrying on with the task of rebalancing the different plant combinations and tracking down lost varieties. With the nursery that they have initiated to sell archetypal Fish plants from a site within the garden, the couple have successfully put in place a further safeguard against the loss of an important contribution to British horticulture.

OPPOSITE
Snowdrops usher in
the early months of the
year at East Lambrook
Manor, here naturalized
with hellebores under
deciduous trees and
(right) on ledges beneath
a witch hazel. The
small, winding stream
was one of Margery
Fish's favourite parts
of the garden.

POSTWAR RESTORATIONS

As in previous wars, most of the fighting during World War I was confined to formalized battle zones, and the physical destruction to property and landscape, although very great, was geographically contained. World War II was different. Civilian populations as well as armies were targeted, and many historic gardens were destroyed. Others not directly affected by warfare were neglected. Therefore, during the postwar decades there was a new incentive for restoration, notably in Germany, Russia, the former Czechoslovakia, and Poland. The results are unfailingly impressive.

Gatchina

ST PETERSBURG • RUSSIA

Gatchina is the least-known of the great royal palaces and gardens around St Petersburg, which include Peter the Great's celebrated summer palace at Peterhof, but in many ways it has one of the most interesting histories. Peter the Great won the area from Sweden in the Great Northern War of 1700–21 and gave Gatchina to his sister, Natasha. Its story as a great garden begins several decades later, with the assassination of Czar Peter III in 1762. The czar was killed at the behest of his German-born wife, who succeeded him to the throne of the Russian empire as Catherine II (later known as Catherine the Great). In 1765, she gave Gatchina to her favourite, Count Grigory Orlov, as a reward for his help in carrying out the *coup d'état* against her husband,

and it was the count who commissioned a palace that ranked as one of the outstanding neoclassical buildings in Russia. The garden that was developed within its spectacular wooded surroundings is credited with being the first of Russia's English-style landscape parks.

European artists and craftsmen had been coming to Russia in increasing numbers since the time of Peter the Great, and Orlov was able to employ an Italian architect, Antonio Rinaldi, to design his palace at Gatchina. Rinaldi used a local limestone that memorably changes hue depending on the sunlight, and he sited the palace overlooking the Silver Lake, which became a focal feature in the 143ha (388 acre) park designed by John Busch.

Originally from Hanover, Busch had lived in London and set up a plant nursery in Hackney before moving to Russia in 1771, when he became Catherine the Great's head gardener and was involved with landscaping her magnificent estate at Tsarskoye Selo. At Gatchina, Busch was assisted by two British gardeners, James Hackett and James Sparrow, plus a workforce of 500. Among the first ornaments to be erected in the park by Orlov, ever loyal to the empress, were the Column of the Eagle and the Chesma Obelisk, built in 1777 to celebrate the imperial navy's recent victory over the Turks.

When Orlov died in 1783, Catherine promptly re-acquired Gatchina and gave it to her son, Grand Duke Paul. The gift was not an act of generosity, however, since its principal aim

was to remove Paul and his wife, Maria Fedorovna, from close proximity to her own favourite palace at Tsarskoye Selo. Paul had pressing worries about his personal safety, owing to the murder of his father and his lifelong feud with his mother, but he felt secure at Gatchina. He transformed Orlov's palace into a more austere-looking fortress and added a number of military touches, such as a parade ground and a moat with a drawbridge.

The extensive formal gardens Paul sited close to the palace were unusual at a time when royal Russian palaces were embracing the landscape garden so enthusiastically. In the private garden created immediately below the windows of Paul's apartment, Italian statues and vases adorned a pattern of topiary and treillage (architectural use of trellis-work), and in the two adjacent Dutch gardens a symmetrical pattern outlined by paths was decorated with statuary and flower parterres. The formal gardens lacked fountains because of problems with harnessing sufficient water pressure, but compensation for this lay in the series of vast lakes and interlinking streams in the wider landscape. The water here is known for its intense clarity, mirroring buildings, trees, and sky.

Paul and his wife travelled regularly to the royal palaces of Europe, in particular to Prussia, France, and Italy, where they gained inspiration for the lavish redecoration of the palace interiors and surrounding gardens. The landscape park laid out by Busch, with paths winding along the lakesides and across bridges to different islands, was enlivened by the addition of buildings such as the Eagle Pavilion; this unusual structure is circular in outline but has a semicircular, roofless colonnade in front and a half dome with a coffered ceiling behind. Paul and Maria Fedorovna were especially enamoured with the Prince de Condé's garden at the Château de Chantilly, in northern France, which they had visited in 1782. They replicated some of its well-known features: the classical Temple of Venus on an

RIGHT
A glimpse of the Priory
Palace, built overlooking
the Black Lake, is visible
beyond the autumn-
tinted lakeside trees.

ABOVE
The Priory Palace
was repaired during
the restoration work
initiated in 1985 to
reverse the landscape's
long-standing decline,
which began when the
royal family ceased
using Gatchina as a
main residence, and
was deepened by
World War II.

Island of Love, and Sylvia, an area of idealized woodland with a network of paths and avenues, next to which was a picturesque farm, or *ferme ornée*, for guests of the imperial family. Also reminiscent of Chantilly was the Birch House, a simple, square construction of birch poles disguising a sophisticated and highly decorated interior.

In 1798, when Paul I had been ruling as czar for two years, he was made Grand Master of the Sovereign Order of the Knights of Malta. It was a position he took seriously, and when his friend the Prince de Condé came to Russia in the aftermath of the French Revolution, Paul made him prior of the Order. It was in the prince's honour that Paul created the unusual Priory Palace overlooking the Black Lake at Gatchina. Its construction of compressed earth fixed to wooden frames with a lime mixture was the work of the influential Russian architect Nikolai Lvov, and has proved extremely durable. Lvov also designed the circular amphitheatre, 60m (200ft) in diameter and surrounded by a raised rampart on which spectators sat. It is presumed that it was designed for contests, but there are no records of any taking place.

After Paul was assassinated in 1801, Gatchina continued to be a much-loved home for Maria Fedorovna, although she also had a deep attachment to her palace at Pavlovsk, built while her husband was still grand duke. In letters to her Pavlovsk gardener, Kuchelbecker, she referred to Gatchina as "a very dangerous rival" and described how a new road running 0.6km (1 mile) around Gatchina's lake was built in a fortnight: "It is a feature of great beauty for Gatchina, but knowing your zeal and your love for Pavlovsk, I am persuaded that you will not remain behind and that I will find wonders on my return. I send you ten roubles so that you can give vodka to the workers in case of need if they get wet" (quoted in Hayden, 2005: 134).

Gatchina fell out of favour as a main residence in the nineteenth century and was used by czars Nicholas I and Alexander II principally for the hunting in the vast surrounding forests. But Alexander III lived here with his family, retreating from St Petersburg partly through fear of the unrest that led to the death of his father in a bomb explosion in 1881, and from 1894 it was a favourite palace of the last czar, Nicholas II. Following the Bolshevik Revolution of October 1917, Prime Minister Aleksandr Kerenski escaped to Gatchina when Lenin overthrew the provisional government, later fleeing to Paris. The palace was made a state museum in 1918, housing an art collection assembled mainly by Paul I, and its future was safeguarded until it became entangled in the events of World War II.

Located 45km (28 miles) south of St Petersburg, Gatchina lay directly on the path of the German army as it advanced towards the city, which was then known as Leningrad. The estate spent more than three years under German occupation, during which time both the palace and gardens were extensively

ABOVE
A plan dating from the early nineteenth century shows how the imposing palace lies at the centre of a landscape notable for the extensive use made of the ornamental possibilities of water. Yet insufficient water pressure meant that the formal gardens never had fountains.

LEFT
The monumental porticoed gateway added in the eighteenth century to adorn one of the park's main entrances was rebuilt following World War II.

damaged, and several of the buildings that adorned the landscape park were destroyed. The art collection that had been removed to safe storage was not brought back to Gatchina once the war was over, and the palace served as a military academy until 1985. The gardens languished during this period, as one observer has recorded: "The palace is surrounded by several beautiful parks, the former grounds of the estate. Unlike the manicured gardens of Peterhof or Tsarskoye Selo, however, these are wild, dotted with wild flowers and the ruins of pavilions, gates, and bridges" (www.themoscowtimes.com).

In 1985, Gatchina became a museum once again, and this change of status marked the beginning of restoration work to the palace and subsequently to the various buildings in the gardens and park. Although it may be less well-known than its famous neighbours at Peterhof, Pavlovsk, or Tsarskoye Selo, Gatchina is equally significant in the development of Russian gardens. Its recent restoration has confirmed its importance and returned life to the largest of St Petersburg's historic landscape gardens.

ABOVE
Among the many and varied ornamental buildings added by Grand Duke Paul and his wife, Maria Fedorovna, was the unusual Eagle Pavilion, shown here in a nineteenth-century watercolour, with the palace in the far distance.

RIGHT
Now restored (minus the eagle) the pavilion has regained its semicircular colonnade and coffered dome.

ABOVE
A pattern of evergreen
hedges is decorated with
statues in one of the
Dutch gardens made
close to the palace for
Grand Duke Paul, whose
tastes were influenced
by visits to the royal
palaces of Europe.

BELOW
Plane trees close to the
palace of Nieborów
shade the patterns of
planting in the restored
parterre, which retains
the spirit of the baroque
garden laid out in the
late seventeenth century.

Nieborów & Arkadia

LOWICZ • POLAND

RIGHT
An early nineteenth-
century plan delineates
the Nieborów
landscape, which from
the 1830s slipped into a
decline lasting for several
decades. Renewed
interest was interrupted
by World War II, but
restoration was under
way by 1948.

BELOW
The garden in the
entrance courtyard
has taken on varying
formal styles since it was
originally designed
in the seventeenth
century for Cardinal
Radziejowski. This
photograph dates from
the first half of the
twentieth century.

By some European standards, the 25ha (62-acre) garden at Nieborów and the adjacent 15ha (37-acre) garden of Arkadia are not on the grandest of scales, but the quantity of decorative buildings and the richness of ornament have made them the focus of periodic restoration from 1948 to the present day. Located close to the town of Lowicz, 80km (50 miles) southwest of Warsaw, the two gardens were already suffering from long-term neglect when they were badly damaged during World War II. Today, by contrast, both present a faithful picture of their heyday in the seventeenth and eighteenth centuries.

The manor house at Nieborów was owned in the late seventeenth century by Cardinal Radziejowski, who commissioned Dutch architect Tylman van Gameren to transform the building into a baroque palace surrounded by suitably formal gardens. When the estate was purchased by Michal Hieronim Radziwill in 1774, he retained the garden's main axis, leading from a parterre in front of the palace to a wide avenue of lime trees, but employed Szymon Bogumil Zug to

BELOW
A view across Zug's
formal canal that bounds
one side of Nieborów's
formal garden.

OPPOSITE
Paths wind through the
numerous woodland
glades surrounding
Nieborów and Arkadia.
Both were influenced by
Polish architect Szymon
Bogumil Zug, who
favoured picturesque
English-style landscapes.

update and expand the gardens. Zug had moved to Poland from his native Saxony in 1756 and became an influential architect in the 1770s–80s. At Nieborów he designed enclosed garden rooms hidden among avenues of hornbeam trees and built the garden's two outstanding classically inspired orangeries. One of the most striking features added was a long, L-shaped canal parallel to the formal gardens. An avenue separated the short arm of the canal from a large lake, and beyond this lay the more natural areas of English-style landscape that Zug favoured.

It was Radziwill's wife, Princess Helena, who was responsible for the creation of the adjoining Arkadia garden, located 4km (2.5 miles) south of Nieborów and connected to it by a path. She began laying out Arkadia in 1778 and while continuing to live in the palace of Nieborów, devoted 40 years of her life to the development of one of the finest landscape gardens in Poland. Her vision of a place for sentimental meditation, set within romantic natural scenery and enlivened with symbolic architecture, was a reaction against the over-decorative baroque style of previous generations. The overall inspiration and scheme were Helena Radziwill's, but she employed Zug as chief architect. Important contributions were also made over the years by a number of other designers and craftsmen.

The fashion for idealized, English-style landscape gardens had already reached other gardens owned by aristocratic families around Warsaw; but it was at Arkadia that Helena Radziwill set a new level of symbolism and iconography, inspired chiefly by the Roman poet Virgil. Her wish to recreate the Arcadian myth explored in his *Eclogues* (42–37 BC) was entirely in keeping

ABOVE
In this wintry view, the portico of Nieborów Palace is just about visible at the far end of the broad lime avenue that has defined the garden's main axis for three centuries.

LEFT
Snow-covered swirls of box hedging animate the parterre at Nieborów. The restoration of this area was guided by eighteenth-century plans and drawings showing the formal layout of the baroque gardens beside the palace.

with contemporary interest in an idealized pastoral landscape. This set of ideas was overlaid by the Renaissance notion of a lost world of perfect happiness and was also combined with reminders of the ever-presence of death.

In his highly influential painting entitled *Et in Arcadia Ego* (1637–38), now in the Louvre museum in Paris, the French painter Nicolas Poussin depicted an idyllic rural scene where shepherds from classical antiquity are gathered around a tomb. Helena Radziwill's Arkadia portrayed a similar theme, in which an emphasis on death and the afterlife governed how the landscape was developed and also influenced the detail of its ornaments and buildings, including their interior decoration. In time, Arkadia became a place of family remembrance. Here Helena Radziwill placed classical urns containing the ashes of her three daughters, all of whom died young, and a memorial to her son in the Knight's Apartment, symbolizing his career as a soldier.

The major structural work needed to create the desired framework for Helena Radziwill's idyllic landscape involved damming the river Lupia to form a large lake. At the same time, hundreds of trees were planted and enormous granite boulders brought in to create a rugged, picturesque effect. The series of buildings that progressively adorned the landscape, each with its own special message and significance, were designed by Zug and a number of other architects; Josef Sierakowski was responsible for some of the most interesting additions. The painters Alekxander Orlowski and Jean-Pierre Norblin decorated the interiors of Zug's buildings, while sculptures were made by Italian artist Gioacchino Staggi.

Among the first embellishments to the landscape was the cascade made where the river flows into the lake, and the cottage sited to overlook it. Next came the High Priest's Sanctuary, an artificial ruin in picturesque style constructed in 1783 using iron ore and stone. It was suitably decorated with Gothic and Renaissance sculptural fragments, including busts displayed on pillars (herms) and grotesque faces carved from keystones (*mascarons*). The garden's most significant building, Zug's classical Temple of Diana, also dates from 1783. A four-columned portico overlooks the lake on one front, while on the other side stands a half-rotunda. The temple was renowned for its interior decoration; the Etruscan room has been restored, but a ceiling painting of the dawn goddess, Aurora, sadly disappeared during a long period of neglect in the nineteenth century.

In common with similar schemes in England, of which Stowe and Stourhead are among the most famous, Arkadia was notable for its variety of architectural style. The Stone Arch was built like an arched bridge for dramatic effect, and a Hermit's Grotto was almost obligatory in such a scheme. Most spectacular of all was the bridge in the form of a two-tiered Roman aqueduct, built over the cascade to Zug's design in 1784. The tomb placed among poplar trees on Topolowa, an artificial island in the middle of the lake, corresponded with the symbolism of Arkadia; it also paid homage to the French author and philosopher Jean-Jacques Rousseau, who died in 1778 and was buried on an island of poplar trees at Ermenonville. Surmounted by an urn, the Topolowa tomb was decorated with a marble relief of the dying Saint Cecilia and bore the Latin inscription *Et in Arcadia Ego* (meaning "I am also in Arcadia," often interpreted as spoken by Death). Because Helena Radziwill planned the tomb for herself, she added a further inscription: *J'ai fait Arcadie, j'y repose* ("I made Arcadia, now I lie there").

From around 1800, additional architectural additions to Arkadia were designed principally by Henryk Ittar. He contributed two of the landscape's most symbolic monuments, the circus and the amphitheatre. Both structures were inspired by the etchings of Giovanni Battista Piranesi, particularly those published in his *Antichità Romane*. Piranesi gained a high reputation in the eighteenth century for his views of Rome and its antiquities and became an important figure in early neoclassicism. Ittar's amphitheatre followed Piranesi's drawings of the theatre at Pompeii, but it was considerably reduced in size and built complete rather than as a part ruin.

The circus is of particular interest, as the Polish historian Wlodzimierz Powkowski has made clear: "The idea of erecting an ancient circus at Arkadia was unprecedented not only in Polish, but also in the whole of modern European architecture" (Powkowski, 1995: 11). Powkowski also explains how the circus completed the ideological scheme of the garden, its ancient use as a place for gladiatorial contests standing as a symbol for the struggle of human existence. The building was sited on the park's central vista, its obelisk on an

BELOW
Arkadia's most famous building, the Temple of Diana, overlooks the lake. It was built in 1783, adding to an ensemble of symbolic architecture, and its much-admired interior decoration has largely been restored.

RIGHT
In this unforgettable section of the High Priest's Sanctuary at Arkadia, ghostly white figures stand between the chunks of iron ore from which it was constructed.

axis with the Temple of Diana and the Stone Arch. Like the amphitheatre, though, the circus is no longer standing.

Helena Radziwill died in 1821, and in the decades following the death of her husband in 1831, both Nieborów and Arkadia fell into decline. There was a revival in fortunes in the late nineteenth to early twentieth centuries, by which time the estate had become the property of another member of the family, politician Janusz Radziwill. He was still its owner at the outbreak of World War II. The family attempted to protect the estate by continuing to live at Nieborów during the war, but Radziwill was arrested by the occupying German forces and held in prison near Berlin for taking part in the Warsaw uprisings of February 1943 and August 1944.

However difficult it must have been, Radziwill had managed to persuade influential friends in Warsaw that Nieborów should become a branch of the city's National Museum. He was supported by Professor Stanislaw Lorentz, then director of the museum, who ensured that the palace and its gardens achieved this status in 1945 – a level of protection that helped the estate survive the turmoil of the postwar period. Radziwill, however, along with his whole family, was arrested in January 1945 by the advancing Russian army and sent to a prison near Moscow. Here his wife died in 1947, and although Radziwill was released and allowed back to Poland some years later, he never returned to Nieborów before his death in 1967.

Even with the efforts of the Radziwill family, World War II brought neglect and devastation to Nieborów and Arkadia. Much of the structure and all the interior of the Temple of Diana were destroyed, and similar damage was caused to other

decorative buildings and ornaments by air raids and military occupation. The gardens were not left long in this state, however, because by 1948 the first of several restoration projects was already under way. The work was led by Gerard Ciolek, the landscape architect and garden historian responsible for most of the major postwar garden restorations in Poland. For Nieborów, Ciolek was guided by the series of eighteenth-century plans and drawings by Zug and so was able to reconstruct the palace's formal baroque garden, with its adjoining canal. During this initial period of work, which was not completed until 1956, Ciolek oversaw repair to the water systems that fed Arkadia's landscape and also the initial restoration of a number of the buildings there.

While one of Zug's two orangeries at Nieborów was rescued during Ciolek's original work in the 1950s, the more beautiful Old Orangery was not restored until the second period of work, which was conducted from 1978 to 1982. Other major projects have included the rebuilding of the Stone Arch in 1993, when the superb relief by Gioacchino Staggi in the High Priest's Sanctuary was also repaired. Perhaps most significant of all was the restoration of the interior of the Temple of Diana.

An exhibition in 2001 celebrated the completion of the most recent phase of restoration and was entitled *Et in Arcadia Ego*. Princess Helena Radziwill's poplar island and its tomb have long since disappeared, but the other major features of her landscape survive in better condition than at any time since she created Arkadia, and its reflective, melancholy atmosphere is still the perfect foil to the more formal picture of Nieborów Palace and its baroque gardens.

ABOVE
Framed by its sylvan setting, the two-tiered Roman aqueduct at Arkadia crosses the river Lupia where it flows into the lake. The bridge dates from the period when Helena Radziwill began creating her idyllic landscape.

Herrenhausen

HANOVER • GERMANY

In 1943, Allied bombing raids on the city of Hanover completely destroyed the royal castle of Herrenhausen and decimated the surrounding Grosser Garten, Germany's greatest baroque garden. Unlike other buildings of historic importance in Germany, the castle was never rebuilt. As a consequence, the enormous garden, which underwent extensive restoration from the 1960s, lacks the architectural focal point that originally gave it purpose. The highly regimented and symmetrical garden was designed in proportion with the castle that once overlooked it. Nonetheless, the monumental restoration of Herrenhausen was one of the most important carried out in postwar Germany.

During the seventeenth century, Herrenhausen was the summer seat of the ruling dukes of Hanover, who from 1708 were elevated to the powerful status of electors to the Holy Roman Empire. The early part of the seventeenth century was dominated by the Thirty Years War, and ambitious gardening plans for Herrenhausen, as for estates across Germany, had to wait until after it ended in 1648. By that time, the fashionable style was the grandiose and formal baroque approach soon to be epitomized by King Louis XIV's celebrated garden at Versailles, in France.

The first garden made at Herrenhausen dates from 1666 and was created by Duke Johann Friedrich. He was a cultivated man influenced by his travels around Venice, and he built a classical "summer house" that overlooked the small garden. In around 1673, the house and garden were both extended under the supervision of Hieronymo Sartorio, a Venetian who was architect to the Hanoverian court. The existing parterre was expanded and given more elaborate decoration, and important architectural features were added, including the cascade and grotto that survive in restored form today.

The chief architect of the main garden, however, was Duke Johann Friedrich's daughter-in-law, Sophie, who was married to the future elector Ernst August. Sophie had been brought up in the Netherlands, where her father Frederick V, the Winter King, lived in exile from Bohemia; it was the Dutch gardens

RIGHT
The restored baroque garden at Herrenhausen, one of the finest in Germany, is overlooked by an orangery that stands alone because the seventeenth-century palace, destroyed in 1943, was never rebuilt.

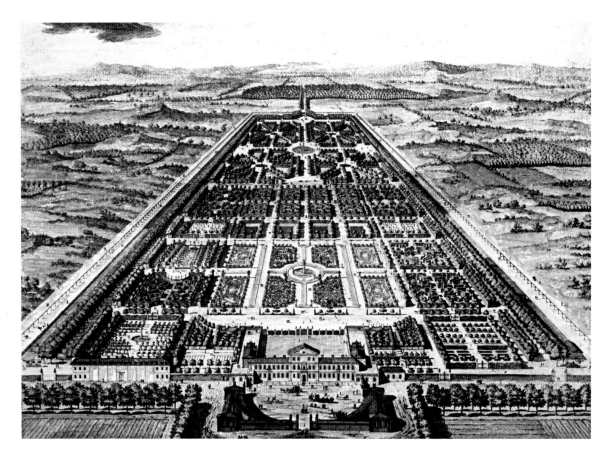

ABOVE
An early eighteenth-century plan illustrates the relationship between the palace at one end and the enormous, symmetrical garden stretching out towards the horizon. The Dutch-style canal enclosing the garden on three sides was the legacy of Electress Sophie's childhood in the Netherlands.

RIGHT
Close to the orangery, citrus trees in terracotta pots decorate a series of checkerboard patterns edged in box.

with which she was familiar that would provide the greatest influence on the garden that she created at Herrenhausen. With the possible exception of the royal garden at Het Loo, Dutch gardens tended to differ from the more ambitious German gardens by their element of intimacy. So, while the Grosser Garten was clearly a garden in the Dutch manner, it was laid out on a much grander scale than was typical in the Netherlands.

Before her marriage, Sophie had lived in Osnabrück, in northwest Germany, and when she moved to Herrenhausen she brought with her the gardener Martin Charbonnier, who had worked at Osnabrück for many years. It was in 1680, at the age of 50, that Sophie began developing and improving the existing garden with Charbonnier's help. She was responsible, in particular, for setting out new groups of sculpture in the large parterre and for trying to improve the performance of the fountains, which, as in the grandest gardens throughout Europe at the time, were a constant problem.

A new phase of work began under Charbonnier's direction after he returned from the Netherlands, where he had been to make a study of gardens. During 1692, the Grosser Garten was virtually doubled in size to its present 50ha (124 acres), by extending an almost square design into a long rectangle enclosed on three sides by a broad canal; the fourth side of the

rectangle was occupied by the palace and its adjacent buildings. The main vistas within the enlarged section of the Grosser Garten, the area known as the New Garden, led through a series of circular or oval *bassins* (formal pools). The largest of these pools was located on the wide, central axis that united the New Garden with the main parterre in front of the palace. Delightful circular pavilions were built in the garden's farthest corners.

When nearing the end of her life, the electress Sophie expressed how important the garden had been to her: *Le jardin de Herrenhausen, qui est ma vie* ("The garden of Herrenhausen, which is my life", quoted in Quest-Ritson, 1998: 124). It was this cultivated princess who undoubtedly played a major part in its development. Within its magnificent overall design, her garden had many notable features: the renowned Hedge Theatre completed in the 1690s; the great fountains in the two pools set on the central axis, and the subtle contrast in shape provided by the smaller octagonal pools in the side areas of the New Garden; and the quality of the statues, vases, and other garden ornaments.

The baroque formality of the garden at Herrenhausen survived more or less intact into the nineteenth century, due mainly to a lack of interest in continuing its development. After Sophie's death in 1714, the court of Hanover moved its base to England, where her son had become King George I. He and his descendants made increasingly infrequent visits and initiated no structural changes to the garden. Perhaps the most significant

developments from the end of the eighteenth century were made by the three generations of the Wendland family that succeeded one another as royal gardeners at Herrenhausen and who introduced a wealth of horticultural rarities.

The first, Johann Christoph Wendland, began work in the gardens in 1778 and remained until a few years before his death in 1828. His grandson, Hermann Wendland, was the most distinguished of the three, being a botanist and horticulturist with a particular interest in tropical palm trees. He made expeditions to South and Central America, Africa, and Australasia, where he discovered new species, and he published the first, definitive monograph on palms. The Peruvian and Brazilian genus *Wendlandiella* was named in his honour.

Much of their work was done in the Berggarten, part of Herrenhausen's original 1660s garden but located on a separate site north of the palace. Sophie had transformed this area into a haven for exotic plants with the addition of a conservatory. During the 1840s, a palm house was designed and built here by architect Georg Ludwig Friedrich Laves (who also designed the mausoleum in the Berggarten, where successive members of the royal family of Hanover were interred). Within five years of its completion in 1849, the glasshouse held the most important collection of palms anywhere in Europe, including the Royal Botanic Gardens at Kew. The Wendlands also introduced a similarly distinguished collection of orchids. The palm house was replaced by an even larger one in 1880, which at a height of 30m (100ft) was the tallest in Europe.

LEFT
To one side of the main parterre lies a large enclosure concealing a yew-hedge maze, while an unusual hedge theatre occupies the same position on the opposite side of the parterre.

OPPOSITE
A pair of circular pavilions with domed roofs was built to mark the far corners of Electress Sophie's garden, in the area where a formal pattern of paths leads between clumps of trees.

During the 1930s, work was carried out to safeguard the gardens at Herrenhausen, and although this was not an attempt at a genuine restoration, some notable new features were added. Most impressive is the Bell Fountain with its 166 jets, placed to occupy a central position within the parterre of the Grosser Garten. In the following decade, however, the garden suffered greatly as a result of wartime bombing. The palm house was hit and demolished in 1944, the year after the castle had been destroyed by British air raids. Architectural structures throughout the garden were extensively damaged, including the formal *bassins*, walls, and paths, as well as the statues, urns, and other ornaments.

Restoration did not begin in earnest until the 1960s, and the postwar decision not to rebuild the castle was adhered to. The only building that now remains to face the enormous formal garden and to play a part in the overall design is the orangery, along with the main staircase leading up to the castle it once stood next to. It is inevitable that a garden of such regimented symmetry, and on an almost completely flat site, lacks an important element without the equally spectacular building that was integral to the original concept. In spite of this loss, the restored Grosser Garten demonstrates the scale, intricacy, and orderliness of a great German baroque garden in the manner that its creators intended.

The restoration work that lies behind this triumph has been painstaking in detail and has taken many decades. Some of the garden's most unusual features have been recreated, including the Hedge Theatre, which is now used regularly for summer productions. It is shaped like a trapezium, and measures 16m (52ft) in width at the front and 8.5m (28ft) at the back. Beech hedges form the wings of the stage, with an orchestra pit in front, and the auditorium is constructed as an amphitheatre. The stone statues that once lined the edges of the auditorium have not been replaced, but the theatre is decorated by replicas of the gilt-lead figures that originally came from the Netherlands.

One of the most memorable features of the Grosser Garten that was damaged during the 1940s was the collection of 32 classical statues that adorned the main parterre. These representations of gods, continents, rivers, and virtues were painted white so that they would stand out against the clipped evergreen hedges and topiary. Virtually none of them survived the war completely unscathed, but they have either been repaired or replaced to demonstrate fully the parterre's ornamental quality. It was a similar story with the restoration of the *bassins* and their fountains, notably the great fountain in the central, circular pool of the New Garden, where the height of the water jet was actually increased to its present limit of 82m (269ft).

Not only is Herrenhausen remarkable for the scale on which it was built, it also has an important place in the history of German gardens. Unlike so many leading German gardens where the baroque style was replaced or diluted by picturesque or English-influenced landscape features, Herrenhausen remained an authentically baroque garden. Its restoration has provided an opportunity to appreciate once again an historical masterpiece from a period that largely vanished after flourishing for a century.

Gilded classical statues emerge onto the stage from the beech-tree wings of the famous Hedge Theatre, which is used for performances in summer. An engraving (right) captures an eighteenth-century view of the same theatre.

ABOVE
Almost none of the main parterre's 32 pieces of sculpture survived World War II intact, but all have been repaired or replaced. True to the originals, they are painted brilliant white and stand out against the greenery.

Neuer Garten

POTSDAM • GERMANY

The Neuer Garten ("New Garden) has a particularly close connection with the events of World War II. As one of a series of royal parks and gardens surrounding the palaces of Potsdam, it suffered extensive damage during the hostilities. Then, in July 1945, with the war in Europe over, the Potsdam Conference between Churchill, Truman, and Stalin was held in the Cecilienhof Palace, located within the Neuer Garten. The conference confirmed the principle of the four-way division of Germany between the occupying powers (Britain, France, the United States, and the Soviet Union) and also led to the cold war, by which Germany was divided for nearly 50 years. The Neuer Garten suffered again in the postwar era, because of its proximity to Berlin: 13ha (32 acres) of the historic landscape along the banks of the river Havel were destroyed or occupied when the Berlin Wall was built by East Germany in 1961, and were returned only in 1990.

It was the picturesque scenery along the river Havel that had attracted the ruling Prussian dynasty of Hohenzollern to Potsdam during the eighteenth century. Frederick the Great had a palace named Sanssouci built to the west of Potsdam in

ABOVE
The Tudor-revival Cecilienhof Palace, surrounded by an English-style flower garden, was built just before World War I. It was the last significant addition made to the Neuer Garten since it was first laid out in 1787.

OPPOSITE
An aerial view of the Cecilienhof shows its sheltered parkland setting towards the northern corner of the Neuer Garten. The palace was chosen in July 1945 as the venue for the Potsdam Conference.

BELOW
This pool and statue
belong to the formal
gardens designed for the
Cecilienhof. The palace
was converted into a
luxury hotel following
restoration in the 1990s.

1745–47 and considered it his favourite home. His son, Frederick William II, who became king of Prussia in 1786, acquired more land in the area and in 1787 commissioned the architect Carl von Gontard to design a palace, the Marmorpalais, east of the town. At the same time, the garden designer Johann August Eyserbeck produced plans for the Neuer Garten, which extended to 121ha (300 acres) between the Heiliger See ("Holy Lake") and the Havel River. It was laid out as a landscape park in the informal English style, as was fashionable at the time, and was decorated with fanciful buildings, including an Egyptian pyramid and a pavilion named the Chinese Parasol.

Alterations to the Neuer Garten during the first half of the nineteenth century, such as a flower parterre added to the front of the Marmorpalais in 1846, were made under the aegis of Peter Joseph Lenné, a landscape gardener and important figure in German garden history. His earliest plans for extensive changes to Sanssouci and the Neuer Garten, drawn up in 1816 when he was a journeyman at Potsdam, were never executed. Over the following 30 years, however, he influenced how the various royal gardens at Potsdam would look for decades to come. As part of his wider initiative to create a vast, connected landscape of parks and palaces, he linked the Neuer Garten with the park he had designed around the Pfingstberg, a hill in the northwest corner of the garden. Lenné was also responsible for landscaping the garden's open spaces, thus creating vistas towards the river and lake.

ABOVE
The Marmorpalais built for Frederick William II of Prussia is seen here beyond the facade of a temple, one of many decorative buildings created for the park during its initial period of development.

LEFT
Stretches of the river Havel have always been one of the great attractions of the Neuer Garten and other royal palaces at Potsdam, which together were declared a UNESCO World Heritage Site in 1990.

By the 1850s, the Neuer Garten had become a place of rich and idiosyncratic charm. From the park gates, which were guarded by lodges in a hybrid of Dutch and Chinese architectural styles, a long avenue of fastigiated oaks passes the Holländisches Etablissement, a collection of gabled cottages suggesting a picturesque Dutch village, before it reaches the Marmorpalais. A ruined temple was placed close to the palace to disguise a kitchen linked to the main building by an underground passage, and a neo-Gothic library set in parkland by the lake complemented a Moorish temple that was situated on the opposite shore.

The last significant addition to the Neuer Garten was a palace, the Cecilienhof, that was commissioned in 1913 by the German emperor William II as a gift for his son, Crown Prince William, and his wife Cecilie. Located in the northern part of the park, the building transformed the priorities of the landscape once it became the main residence within the grounds. Although it was given its own flower garden, the palace remained shrouded in the mature trees of the surroundings in order to retain an atmosphere of quiet seclusion. In its resemblance to an English neo-Tudor country house, the Cecilienhof continued the theme of architectural variety that characterizes the Neuer Garten. With its tall chimneys and gables, half-timbered walls, and leaded windows, the palace was a replica of the Arts and Crafts houses that Kaiser William II admired when visiting his grandmother, Queen Victoria, in England.

The outbreak of World War I in 1914 did not immediately affect the occupants of the Cecilienhof, and even after the

ruling family was deposed in 1918 and replaced by the government of the Weimar Republic, the Neuer Garten was not confiscated by the state until the beginning of World War II. Although the Cecilienhof was in a good enough state of repair to host the Potsdam Conference in 1945, extensive damage to the surrounding landscape was compounded by the detonation of unexploded bombs, one of which destroyed an ornamental bridge. The Neuer Garten disappeared from sight as a historic garden during the period it served as the East German headquarters of the Soviet Union's security police, the KGB.

The interconnected complex of Potsdam gardens and palaces planned by Lenné was designated a UNESCO World Heritage Site in 1990, since which time the Neuer Garten has re-emerged from obscurity. The Cecilienhof was converted into a luxury hotel, the buildings in the park were restored, and replanting was carried out. The Neuer Garten is today perhaps the most popular public garden in Potsdam, where visitors can enjoy the parkland's tranquil open spaces, the revived Lenné flower parterre, tropical plants inside the Egyptian-style orangery, as well as the restored English-style herbaceous borders in the courtyards of the Cecilienhof. It is hard to believe that the dark era of the cold war was set in motion by a meeting of the Allied leaders within the cosy walls of the garden's neo-Tudor palace.

GENUINE, NOT PASTICHE

The evidence of such internationally acclaimed restorations as Colonial Williamsburg in the United States, or Château de Courances in France suggests that successful restoration is anything *but* pastiche. For more than a century, we have increasingly come to value the treasures of the past and are fascinated by the artistic and practical skills with which they were created. Casting aside any emotional aspect, it is clear that restoration aids our ability to appreciate the tastes and techniques of previous generations. This is ultimately what makes restoration so fascinating, valuable, and justifiable.

BIDDULPH GRANGE

When the National Trust completed restoration of the Victorian garden at England's Biddulph Grange, having acquired the Staffordshire property in 1988, the response among some of the gardening cognoscenti was not entirely positive. At a cost of more than £5 million (US$9.9 million), this was the most expensive garden restoration project the trust had ever undertaken and there were concerns that it had produced nothing more than a gaudy pastiche. The 6ha (15-acre) garden had been created by James Bateman in the 1840s–70s, with the help of his wife, Maria, and artist Edward Cooke, and it was hard to believe that Bateman could ever have intended it to look quite so theatrical.

The doubts did not last long. The National Trust had marshalled impressive quantities of historical evidence during its detailed research into the original appearance of the garden. A wealth of written and photographic material had survived from the Victorian period, supplemented by an informative record of the garden's decline from the 1920s onwards. Fortunately, even though the garden was vandalized after it became derelict, many of the original features remained in place, unmodified.

BELOW
One of the most skilful elements of the National Trust's work at Biddulph Grange was its exact recreation of the downward-sloping Dahlia Walk, a high-maintenance feature that was abandoned in the 1920s.

OPPOSITE
The wooden Chinese Bridge had collapsed during the garden's decline, but after it was rebuilt using fragments from the original framework, it looked as brilliantly new as when first constructed in the Victorian era.

The National Trust could simply have decided to put an end to the garden's decline and safeguard its future. It embarked instead upon a total restoration of a kind that had hardly been contemplated anywhere before. Bateman's original would be recreated in minute detail, even if the quest for historical authenticity meant testing a huge range of paints in order to reproduce just the right brilliant red needed for the Chinese Bridge. The revived garden would reveal aspects of Victorian culture that Bateman had embraced, such as the excited acquisitiveness for unusual and newly discovered plants shown by the avenue of Wellingtonias (*Sequoiadendron giganteum*, introduced to Europe from California in 1853). Bateman arranged his garden with different areas exploring the flora of

China, Egypt, and other parts of the world. In the shady dell that he turned into a stumpery, using arrangements of picturesque old tree roots, and in the series of dark passages leading through great blocks of stone, Bateman also expressed the Victorian love of the kind of chilling fantasy American author Edgar Allan Poe portrayed in his short stories.

As the National Trust began the restoration, fundamental decisions had to be made about whether to recreate missing parts of the garden, including the formal parterres and sunken Dahlia Walk. As National Trust garden expert Bill Malecki has explained, these small areas were a distinctive part of Bateman's scheme: "Certainly, their recreation ... meant a significant additional maintenance burden (the reason they had been destroyed in the 1920s) but otherwise the garden would have remained an impoverished version of the original" (Calnan, 2001: 55).

Other features presented different challenges. Wooden structures, such as the temple and bridge in the area known as "China", had largely rotted away, but segments surviving from the originals were saved and incorporated, even though this made the restoration work more complicated. The Wellingtonia avenue presented a difficult dilemma, given that gaps had appeared at different times and no amount of filling-in with replacement trees would recapture the desired impact. As a result, the decision was taken to cut down all the surviving trees and replant the whole avenue: controversial, but unquestionably in the best interests of the garden.

Biddulph Grange is today one of the National Trust's most popular gardens. It provides a rare insight into a mid-Victorian style of gardening that disappeared when its complex, eclectic mixture of exotic planting and ornament heavy with significance was replaced by the late-nineteenth-century preference for classicism and naturalism. It is also testament to the exhaustive research and uncompromising decisions that lie behind the restoration.

MOUNT VERNON

Whenever he was away from the turmoil of war and politics, George Washington's two great passions were farming and gardening. Indeed, it is one of the enduring qualities of the United States' first great statesmen that behind his extraordinary career as soldier and politician lay a deep-rooted interest in all aspects of his native country. His home at Mount Vernon, located 24km (15 miles) south of Washington DC in the state of Virginia, has one of the best-documented gardens in American history, matched only by the garden made by fellow statesman Thomas Jefferson. This unusually comprehensive body of written and pictorial evidence formed the basis of the garden restoration undertaken in the twentieth century by the Mount Vernon Ladies Association, which had acquired the property with great foresight in 1858.

As a place that was loved by the man who was a leading opponent of British rule in the American colonies, who served as commander-in-chief during the American Revolution of 1775–83, and who in 1789 became the very first president of the United States, Mount Vernon was preserved as a tribute to Washington's achievements. Washington was born into a wealthy Virginia family in 1732, and in 1761 inherited the 3,200ha (8,000-acre) agricultural estate that was founded in the 1670s by his ancestors when they emigrated to America from Europe.

Washington's love of farming, gardening, and architecture underlay the energy with which he set about transforming his family home into a house and garden idyll. The original modest farmhouse was replaced by a larger house in classical style, and areas of park were laid out to make the most of views across the Potomac River. The scenery facing the eastern side of the house was described with enthusiasm by an English visitor,

OPPOSITE
Every carefully researched detail of the restoration contributed to the authentic finish it achieved, right down to the type of paint used to complete the temple in this area representing the flora of China.

ABOVE
The restored estate at
Mount Vernon embodies
George Washington's
interest in farming and
gardening as much as it
pays tribute to his role
in American history.
Here, the walled kitchen
garden demonstrates
Washington's emphasis
on productivity.

RIGHT
The flower borders
have been replanted
exactly as they were in
the 1790s, drawing on
Washington's many
letters and the memoirs
of contemporary
visitors. The twin
pepper-pot pavilions
were originally built to
house tools and seeds.

William Loughton Smith, in 1791: "From the grand portico which fronts the river, the assemblage of objects is grand beyond description, embracing the magnificence of the river with the vessels sailing about; the verdant fields, woods and parks" (quoted in Martin, 1991: 142).

Washington designed the 200ha (500-acre) landscape himself, no doubt making use of skills he had learned as a surveyor before his military career began. Behind the house to the west, the principal garden was restricted to two walled areas: one for flowers and the other for fruit and vegetables. Known as the North Garden and the South Garden, they were placed on either side of the pair of curving drives that wound up to the house from the entrance gate. Washington demonstrated his horticultural knowledge and enthusiasm for native American species by planting shrubberies and groves of trees along the drives, concealing the house to provide an element of surprise.

Washington was often away from Mount Vernon and referred to the garden in regular correspondence with his overseer, Anthony Whiting. Washington's letters have yielded valuable information for the restoration, especially concerning the plants he grew. The observations recorded by visitors have also proved useful. A plan of the house and garden sketched in 1787 by an English friend, Samuel Vaughan, shows a central pear-shaped bowling lawn encircled by curving shrubberies, lying in the area between the formally shaped and planted walled gardens.

A similar view of the garden is given by Benjamin Latrobe, the French-born American architect best-known for his design of the Capitol Building in Washington DC. He painted two watercolours of the house in 1796, three years before Washington's death. He wrote: "The ground on the west front of the house is laid out in a level lawn bounded on each side with a wide but extremely formal serpentine walk, shaded by weeping Willows ... On one side of this lawn is a plain kitchen garden, on the other a neat flower garden laid out in squares" (quoted in Martin, 1991: 137–8). Some of the garden's construction and planting details were recorded in 1798 by a Polish visitor, Julian Niemcewicz. He describes how the west garden was "surrounded by a ditch in brick with very pretty little turrets at the corners", and observes that "near the two ends of the house are planted two groves of acacia" (quoted in Martin, 1991: 140).

A wealth of evidence was brought to bear in the restoration work carried out by the Mount Vernon Ladies Association after the property was designated a National Historic Landmark in 1960. The pair of pepper-pot pavilions mentioned by Niemcewicz, which Washington designed for the corners of the flower and vegetable gardens, are today used for storing tools and seeds, just as intended. The plants in the garden and grounds are, as far as possible, those that Washington is known to have cultivated here, and the fruit and vegetables, while no longer grown to feed the people living on the estate, continue to reflect the eighteenth-century emphasis on productivity.

RIGHT
Ornamental trees punctuate the well-tended areas of lawn that once again surround the eastern colonnaded front of the house. In Washington's day, the house was admired for its fine views over the Potomac River.

COLONIAL WILLIAMSBURG

The 10-year garden restoration programme that began in Williamsburg during the 1920s was one of the earliest attempts to restore and preserve a group of urban gardens representing a bygone community. The small town of Williamsburg was the capital of the prosperous and sophisticated colony of Virginia from 1699 to 1781, during a formative time in the establishment and growth of the American colonies. In the early years of the eighteenth century, Williamsburg's first governor, Francis Nicholson, set out a detailed town plan in a series of written instructions that determined the position and size of public buildings and housing for ordinary citizens. Domestic gardens were limited by Nicholson's stipulations to 0.4ha (one acre) of land, clearly differing in status from the extensive grounds surrounding the Governor's Palace.

The arrangement of buildings laid out according to Nicholson's plan survived into the twentieth century, with houses still in their original positions. Although the houses had been rebuilt, and physical evidence of the earliest gardens had almost all disappeared, it was clear that Williamsburg presented a rare opportunity to restore a connected group of buildings and, at the same time, to recreate an accurate picture of the Anglo-Dutch style that prevailed in early colonial gardens. Generously financed by John D Rockefeller Jr, and managed in the early years by landscape architect Arthur Shurcliff, the restoration was one of the first in the world to be based on extensive research. Archaeological surveys revealed long-concealed walkways that were restored as paths and boundaries, thus reconstructing the outlines of the gardens. Contemporary documents were scoured for useful information, such as the tax records that revealed the proportions of some properties. On a practical level, the focus was on returning the gardens to their eighteenth-century design, which typically included small boxwood parterres, or fruit trees and vegetables, with ornamental details such as low fences and brick paths.

While significant in its own right, the restoration also influenced American garden design in the 1930s and 1940s by stimulating an awareness and appreciation of early colonial gardens and giving rise to a style termed "colonial revival". And in the field of garden restoration, Williamsburg has been the subject of a wider, continuing debate: how "genuine" can the restoration claim to be? The techniques used were advanced for the time, but right from the outset questions were raised about whether authenticity could really be achieved. Colonial Williamsburg has since been described as "a compromise between historical authenticity and common sense, between brutal realism and gentle ambience, between being a moment of time in the eighteenth century and being nearly 300 years old" (Brinkley & Chappell, 1996: 4). Retrospective evaluations such as this are not only fascinating; they are an integral part of the restoration process, which inevitably reflects the methods and views of the era in which it was carried out.

RIGHT
A core of buildings surviving from the town's colonial past was the focus of a pioneering restoration in the 1920s. It set new standards at the time and, incidentally, created a revival of interest in colonial-style gardening.

LEFT
White picket fencing, typical of the Anglo-Dutch domestic gardens of eighteenth-century Williamsburg, surrounds a blend of flowers, herbs, and vegetables appropriate to the period. Such attention to detail is a sign of authenticity, even if the restoration feels slightly staged overall.

VILLA D'ESTE

The Villa d'Este in Tivoli has been in the spotlight from the time it was created for Cardinal Ippolito II d'Este in the mid-sixteenth century. Arguably the most famous garden of the Italian Renaissance, it is a UNESCO World Heritage Site. The key work, in particular the design of the fountains and aqueduct, was by the brilliant painter, architect, and engineer Pirro Ligorio.

It was during the eighteenth century that the waterworks ceased to operate, statues were removed, and the villa was left abandoned. By the following century, the garden had an atmosphere of romantic decay that some commentators felt was appropriate. Italian garden historian Isa Belli Barsali described its "special beauty made up of different layers laid down over the course of time"; and although the design's main axes were obscured by vegetation, she warned against "obliterating the most recent states in order, as happens in architecture, to restore false ones" (Mosset & Teyssot, 1991: 528).

Villa d'Este became a national monument under state ownership at the outbreak of World War I, when a policy of limited management was deemed insufficient. The garden's status demanded that its fountains should be made operative. Restoration started in the 1920s, when the garden opened to the public, but bombing during World War II brought further damage. A more extensive restoration programme began in the 1940s, and has continued periodically since. Without it, we would have lost one of the most sublime gardens ever created.

OPPOSITE
Even though many commentators felt it was best to leave Villa d'Este enveloped in the atmosphere of romantic neglect that had intensified during the nineteenth century, their doubts were eventually outweighed by the case in favour of reviving the garden's Renaissance splendour.

BELOW
Hidden behind the powerful performance of the villa's unforgettable fountains is a modern system controlling the flow of water and ensuring its distribution throughout the garden.

CHÂTEAU DE COURANCES

The garden at the Château de Courances, located 61km (31 miles) south of Paris, has undergone two major periods of restoration in the twentieth century, the most recent of which was a response to damage caused during World War II. The previous restoration was carried out in the years leading up to World War I and has been criticized by some garden historians as artificial for the way it reproduced the seventeenth century design originally laid out to complement the moated château largely built earlier the same century.

The garden took its theme from the abundance of water supplied by 11 natural springs, considered so pure that the water was reputedly transported to nearby Fontainebleau for the king's children to drink. The garden's original design, grand but elegant, is attributed to Jean Le Nôtre (father of André Le Nôtre). It was characterized by a series of long, broad canals that reflected the green foliage of flanking avenues and clipped hedges, some planted close to the water and others set back from it, standing majestically behind stretches of lawn.

The property fell into decline during the nineteenth century, and when Jules Le Coeur visited in 1866 with the painters Renoir and Sisley, he commented with some approval: "such a beautiful abandoned château ... surrounded by water and not kept up, gradually subsiding like a sugar-lump melting away in a damp corner" (quoted in Taylor, 1998: 62). Courances was purchased six years later by Baron Samuel de Haber. He employed the fashionable French architect, Gabriel Hippolyte Destailleurs, for extensive restoration work to the château and

BELOW
Courances evolved into a romantically overgrown state until Achille Duchêne was commissioned to recreate the formal seventeenth-century gardens. His work here, including immaculate parterres laid out on their former site beside the moat, is universally applauded.

some alterations to the garden, in particular turning part of it into an informal, landscaped *jardin à l'anglaise*.

Two generations later, Courances had descended through Baron de Haber's daughter to the de Ganay family. The Marquis de Ganay and his wife employed Achille Duchêne, the best-known French garden designer of the late nineteenth century and a specialist in historical restorations of classic gardens, to recreate a formal water garden in late seventeenth-century style. He swept away the *jardin à l'anglaise* and, using the remaining outline of the old formal garden, he revived the framework of parterres, canals, and avenues.

When the château was occupied during World War II, first by the Germans and then the Americans; military buildings were dotted about in the grounds and the entire garden fell into disrepair once again. Slow, painstaking work by the de Ganay family has brought the garden back to its pre-war condition. Visitors today are greeted by an avenue of ancient plane trees dating from 1782, and stroll along it towards the chateau. Here they discover the double *parterre de broderie*, with swirling patterns of clipped box, before moving to the tranquil combination of trees and water in the gardens beyond. Many find Château de Courances to be a remarkably beautiful and memorable place, and the fact that the formal water garden in reality dates from the early twentieth century does not detract from its impact, or from the quality of Duchêne's masterly work – which undoubtedly captures the essence of the place.

ABOVE
Water underlies the abiding beauty of the garden at Château de Courances, where trees are mirrored on the surface of long, broad canals. The water features were created by harnessing the site's natural springs.

Gazetteer of Gardens

CZECH REPUBLIC
Lednice and Valdice, Lednice
Tel: + 420 519 340 112
www.lednice.cz

ENGLAND & WALES
Aberglasney, Carmarthenshire
Tel: + 44 (0) 1558 668 998
www.aberglasney.org

Biddulph Grange, Staffordshire
Tel: + 44 (0) 1782 517999
e-mail:biddulphgrange@nationaltrust.org.uk

Brodsworth Hall, Yorkshire
Tel + 44 (0) 1302 722598
www.english-heritage.org.uk

East Lambrook Manor, Somerset
Tel: + 44 (0) 1460 240328
www.eastlambrook.co.uk

Hampton Court, Middlesex
Tel: + 44 (0) 208 781 9509
www.hrp.org.uk

Heligan, Cornwall
Tel: + 44 (0) 1726 845100
www.heligan.com

Painswick, Gloucestershire
Tel: + 44 (0) 01452 813204
www.rococogarden.co.uk

Upton Grey, Hampshire
Tel: + 44 (0)1256 862827
uptongrey.garden@lineone.net
www.gertrudejekyllgarden.co.uk

Westbury Court, Gloucestershire
Tel: + 44 (0)1452 760461
westburycourt@nationaltrust.org.uk

FRANCE
Château de Marqueyssac, Dordogne
www.marqueyssac.com

Château de Courances, Île de France
Tel: + 33 (0) 1 64 98 41 18
www.courances.net

Château de Vaux-le-Vicomte, Seine et Marne
Tel: + 33 (0) 1 64 14 41 90
www.vaux-le-vicomte.com

Château de Villandry, Tours
Tel: + 33 (0) 2 47 50 02 09
www.chateauvillandry.com

Serre de la Madone, Menton
www.serredelamadone.com

GERMANY
Augustusberg, Cologne
Tel: + 49 (0) 22 32 440 00
www.schlossbruehl.de

Neuer Garden, Potsdam
Tel: + 49 (0) 3319 694 246
www.spsg.de

Herrenhausen, Hanover
Tel: +49 (0) 511 16847743
www.hannover.de/herrenhausen/index.html

ITALY
Villa d'Este, Tivoli
Tel: + 39 (0) 774 312070
info@villadestetivoli.info

Villa Farnese, Caprarola
Tel: + 39 07 61 64 60 52

Villa la Pietra
Open by appointment
Fax to: + 39 (0) 55 472 725

MOROCCO
La Majorelle
Tel: + 212 (0) 24 30 18 52
www.jardinmajorelle.com

THE NETHERLANDS
Het Loo, Apeldoorn
www.paleishetloo.nl

PAKISTAN
Shalimar Bagh, Lahore
www.lahore.gov.uk

POLAND
Nieborów and Arkadia, Lowicz
nieborow@smelcom.lowicz.pl

RUSSIA
Gatchina, St Petersburg
Tel: + 7 (812) 71 134492

Peterhof, St Petersburg
Tel: + 7 (812) 420 0073
www.peterhof.org

SPAIN
Carmen de los Martires, Granada
Tel: + 34 958 227 953
informacion@granada.org

UNITED STATES
Colonial Williamsburg, Virginia
Tours open to visitors
www.history.org

Garland Farm, Maine
Open by appointment
Visit@BeatrixFarrand.org

Kaufmann "Desert House", California
Not open to visitors

Lyndhurst, New York State
Tel: + 1 914 631 4481
www.lyndhurst.org

Montgomery Place, New York State
Tel: + 1 914 631 8200
www.hudsonvalley.org/montgomeryplace/
index.htm

The Mount
Tel: + 1 413 637 1899
www.edithwharton.org

Mount Vernon, Virginia
Tel: + 1 703 780 2000
www.mountvernon.org

Stan Hywet Hall, Ohio
Tel: + 1 330 836 5533
www.stanhywet.org

Sunnyside, New York State
Tel: + 1 914 631 8200
www.hudsonvalley.org/sunnyside/index.htm

Biographies

Acton, Arthur (1873–1953)
Anglo-Italian art connoisseur who purchased Villa la Pietra with his wealthy American wife, Hortense, restored the villa and created the present garden.

Acton, Sir Harold (1904–94)
Aesthete son of Arthur Acton who inherited and lived at Villa la Pietra and bequeathed it to New York University.

Bateman, James (1812–97)
Victorian owner of Biddulph Grange who, with his wife, Maria, created the garden at Biddulph Grange, helped by their friend, marine artist Edward Cooke.

Bush (Busch), John (c.1730–c.90)
English gardener who was born in Germany, left England to go to Russia, and worked as a landscape gardener for Catherine the Great, principally at Tsarskoye Selo; he also designed the park at Gatchina for Count Orlov. He was succeeded by his son. His daughter married Catherine's architect, Charles Cameron.

Caratti, Francesco (c.1615-20–1677)
Italian-born architect who was one of the most important figures in the seventeenth-century baroque movement in Bohemia (later the Czech Republic). Designed the original Baroque palace at Lednice with Tencalla.

Carvallo, Dr Joachim (1869–1936)
Spanish-born doctor who purchased Château de Villandry in 1906 and restored the château and gardens. In 1924, he founded Le Demeure Historique, a group for the owners of historically important châteaux.

Cecilie, Princess of Germany (1886–1954)
Wife of Crown Prince William, son of Kaiser William II of Germany, after whom the Cecilienhof at the Neuer Garten was named and where the 1945 Potsdam Conference took place.

Charbonnier, Martin (active 1660–90)
French gardener who trained under André Le Nôtre. Employed by Electress Sophie of Hanover to design the Grosser Garten at Herrenhausen from 1682.

Clément, Gilles (1943–)
French garden designer who oversaw the restoration of Serre de la Madone.

Conde, Louis Joseph, Prince de (1736–1818)
Friend of Grand Duke Paul and his wife, Maria Fedorovna, whose garden at Chantilly strongly influenced their work at Gatchina.

Davis, Alexander Jackson (1803–92)
Regarded as the most senior American architect of his generation. Architect of the two Hudson River houses, Lyndhurst and Montgomery Place.

De Cerval, Julien (c.1830–c.90)
Owner of Château de Marqueyssac. Created the terraced garden with boxwood parterres from 1863 when he inherited the property.

De Ganay, Ernest (1880–1963)
French writer, gardener, and garden designer, friend of Lawrence Johnston.

De Haber, Baron Samuel (active 1872–1884)
Swiss banker who bought Château de Courances in 1872 and carried out restoration that was continued by his granddaughter and her husband, the Marquis de Ganay.

Delafield, Violetta (1875–1949)
Wife of John Ross Delafield, who owned the Hudson River property Montgomery Place. A keen horticulturist and gardener who was responsible for much of the garden's planting.

D'Este, Cardinal Ippolito II (1509–72)
Renaissance patron of the arts who commissioned Pirro Ligorio to create the gardens of the Villa d'Este.

Destailleurs, Gabriel Hippolyte (1822–93)
French neo-Renaissance architect renowned for his restoration work at châteaux, including Courances and Vaux-le-Vicomte.

Downing, Andrew Jackson (1815–52)
American landscape designer and garden writer who had a strong influence on gardens along the Hudson River and who went into partnership with Andrew Jackson Davis, the architect of Lyndhurst and Montgomery Place.

Duchêne, Henry (1835–c.1900) **and Achille** (1866–1947)
Father and son garden designers who worked especially on historical restorations in France. Achille Duchêne restored the gardens of Château de Courances and Château de Vaux-le-Vicomte.

Eyserbeck, Johann August (c.1740–c.1820)
Garden designer employed by Frederick William II at Neuer Garten, Potsdam, Germany.

Farnese, Cardinal Alessandro II (1520–89)
Cardinal and papal diplomat, and patron of the arts who commissioned Vignola at Villa Farnese.

Farrand, Beatrix (1872–1959)
One of America's most renowned garden designers of the twentieth century, who made her last garden at her home, Garland Farm, in Maine.

Fish, Margery (1888–1969)
Popular English garden writer who created the revered cottage garden at East Lambrook Manor.

Fouquet, Nicolas (1615–80)
French finance minister under Louis XIV who created the château and gardens at Vaux-le-Vicomte, which provoked Louis into outdoing them at Versailles. Fouquet was imprisoned and died in disgrace.

Frederick William II, King of Prussia
Son of Frederick the Great who acquired land at Potsdam, where he began the landscape of Neuer Garten.

Frederick William IV, King of Prussia (1770–1840)
Great nephew of Frederick the Great who commissioned important alterations to the gardens of Augustusburg, Cologne.

Gerard, Dominique (active c.1727–28)
Designed the original parterre garden at Augustusburg, Cologne.

Gould, Jay (1836–92)
Financier, railroad developer, and speculator, and owner of Lyndhurst.

Hanover, Johann Friedrich, Duke of (1607–92)
Creator of first garden at Herrenhausen, Hanover.

Hanover, Sophie, Electress of (1630–1714)
Daughter-in-law of Duke Joseph, wife of his son Ernst August, elector of Hanover and mother of King George I of England. She was responsible for the main development of the Grosser Garten at Herrenhausen, Hanover.

Hardtmuth, Joseph (1758–1816)
Austrain-born architect who designed a number of the buildings in the park of Lednice, Lowicz, Poland.

Hobhouse, Penelope (b.1929–)
Adviser to restoration project at Aberglasney and designer of the planting in the walled garden.

Irving, Washington (1783–1859)
Popular American author and owner of Sunnyside on the Hudson River, New York.

Ittar, Henryk (active c.1820)
Architect and garden designer responsible for changes and additions to garden and architecture at Arkadia, Lowicz, Poland, during the early nineteenth century.

Jekyll, Gertrude (1843–1932)
British garden designer and writer who was responsible for the original design and planting and the Manor House, Upton Grey, Hampshire.

Johnston, Lawrence (1871–1958)
American-born garden owner, plantsman, and plant collector who designed the garden of Serre de la Madone.

Kaufmann, Edgar J (1885–1955)
American businessman and philanthropist from Pittsburg who commissioned the Kaufmann "Desert House".

Kornhäusel, Joseph (active c.1820)
Austrian-born architect who designed a number of the buildings at Lednice, in the Czech Republic.

Le Blond, Jean-Baptiste (1679–1719)

French-born architect and garden designer who studied under André Le Nôtre. In 1716, he went to St Petersburg where he worked for Peter the Great; his outstanding work was done at Peterhof before his early death three years later.

Le Brun, Charles (1619–90)

French artist, principally a painter, but who gained control of the decorative and ornamental schemes in the gardens of Château de Vaux-le-Vicomte and subsequently at Versailles.

Le Nôtre, André (1613–1700)

French garden designer who first trained as a painter before succeeding his father in charge of the Tuileries. The most influential garden designer in Europe of the baroque period, responsible for the gardens at Versailles. Prior to Versailles he created the gardens at Château de Vaux-le-Vicomte.

Le Vau, Louis (1612–70)

French architect who worked closely with André Le Nôtre to produce the French style that unified a palace and its surrounding gardens, as they achieved at Château de Vaux-le-Vicomte and then at Versailles.

Lenné, Peter Josef (1789–1866)

Leading German garden designer of the early nineteenth century, responsible for extensive plans for alterations at Neuer Garten, only some of which were carried out.

Ligorio, Pirro (c.1510–83)

Architect, garden designer, and engineer who created the gardens of the Villa d'Este, Tivoli.

Majorelle, Jacques (1886–1962)

Artist and son of famous art nouveau furniture designer, Louis Majorelle, who moved to Marrakech and created the garden of La Majorelle.

Manning, Warren (1860–1938)

Landscape architect and garden designer who trained in the office of Frederick Law Olmsted and designed parts of the garden at Stan Hywet Hall.

Maria Fedorovna, grand duchess of Russia (1759–1828)

German-born princess whose husband became Czar Paul I of Russia but only reigned for five years before he was murdered and succeeded by their son, Alexander I. Maria Fedorovna was influential in the design of the gardens and landscape at Gatchina.

Marot, Daniel (1661–1752)

French Huguenot gardener who fled France in 1685 for the Netherlands, where he became garden designer to William III. He was the central figure in the development of the Dutch baroque garden from French gardens, exemplified at Het Loo. He also worked for William III at Hampton Court Palace, where he designed the Great Fountain Garden.

Martinelli, Domenico (1650–1719)

Italian-born architect who worked at Lednice, in the Czech Republic, during the early eighteenth century.

Meersmans, Hubert (active c.1900)

Belgian-born businessman who purchased Carmen de los Martires in Spain and was primarily responsible for creating the gardens.

Moggridge, Hal (b.1936–)

Landscape and garden designer, adviser to the restoration project at Aberglasney, Wales, and designer of the restored pool garden there.

Neutra, Richard (1892–1970)

Leading modernist architect who was born in Austria but became an American citizen and worked mainly in California. Designer of the Kaufmann "Desert House".

Newton, Ernest (1856–1922)

English architect who belonged to a group who admired the English Renaissance style and were close to the Arts and Crafts Movement. Designer of the manor house Upton Grey, Hampshire.

Orlov, Count Grigory (1734–1783)

Russian soldier and politician, favourite of Catherine the Great, who gave him the property of Gatchina.

Paul, Grand Duke and later czar of Russia (1754–1801)

Son of Catherine the Great and responsible for most of garden and park features at Gatchina, which was his favourite home.

Peter the Great, Czar of Russia (1672–1725)

Russian emperor who commissioned the gardens at Peterhof to confirm Russia's achievement of sophistication as a European nation.

Radziwill, Princess Helena (c.1750–1821)

Creator of the allegorical landscape garden at Arkadia, Lowicz, Poland.

Rainaldi, Girolamo (1570–1655)

Mannerist Italian architect who worked at Villa Farnese.

Rinaldi, Antonio (1710–94)

Italian-born architect of the Russian palace of Gatchina for Count Orlov.

Robins, Thomas (1716–70)

English artist whose view of Painswick was the basis of the garden restoration there.

Roman, Jacob (1640–1716)

Dutch architect and sculptor who was largely responsible for the design of the palace and gardens at Het Loo, the Netherlands, where the classical plan was embellished by Daniel Marot's decorations.

Rockefeller, John D (1839–1937)

American industrialist and oil magnate who became recognized as the founder of modern philanthropy. The restoration of Sunnyside and Colonial Williamsburg were both projects that he closely supported.

Rudd, Bishop Anthony (c.1548–c.1615)

Bishop of St David's, Wales, who was responsible for the original garden at Aberglasney.

Saint Laurent, Yves (b.1936)

French-born fashion designer who restored the garden of La Majorelle, Morocco.

Schinkel, Karl Frederick (1781–1841)

Architect and urban planner who was involved in the emergence of the public garden movement in Germany and who worked closely with Peter Josef Lenné. Schinkel designed the temple of Pomona in the Neuer Garten, Potsdam.

Shah Jahan (1592–1666)

Fifth Mughal emperor who created the garden of Shalimar Bagh, Lahore.

Shipman, Ellen Biddle (1869–1960)

American-born garden designer who designed the English Garden at Stan Hywet Hall, Ohio.

Seiberling, Franklin A (1859–1955)

American businessman and founder of the Goodyear Tire company who commissioned the Arts and Crafts house and garden at his home, Stan Hywet Hall.

Shurcliff, Arthur (1865–1957)

American landscape architect who was retained to oversee the initial restoration of Colonial Williamsburg between the two world wars.

Smit, Tim (b.1954–)

Entrepreneur and conservationist who organized the restoration of Heligan and then created the Eden Project in Cornwall.

Sommier, Alfred (c.1820–1908)

French businessman who purchased Château de Vaux-le-Vicomte at public auction in 1875 and restored the château and gardens.

Suarez, Diego (c.1895–c.1960)

Colombian-born garden designer trained by Arthur Acton at Villa la Pietra, Italy.

Tencalla, Giovanni Giacomo (c.1610–c.80)

Swiss-born architect who was leading figure in early baroque movement in Moravia and Bohemia (later the Czech Republic) and who, with Caratti, designed the original palace at Lednice.

Tijou, Jean (fl.1689–1711)

French-born ironworker, acknowledged as the outstanding craftsman in this field of his generation, who worked in England and created the great screen of decorative panels at Hampton Court.

Tuvolkov, Vasily (fl.1710–30)

Russian hydraulic engineer who was responsible for the engineering that produced the waterworks at Peterhof for Peter the Great.

Vignola, Giacomo Barozzi da (1507–73)

Italian architect who had profound influence on Italian gardens of the Italian Renaissance through his design of the Caprarola garden at Villa Farnese as well as the design of the nearby Villa Lante garden.

Van Gameren, Tylman (1632–1706)

Dutch architect who spent most of his life in Poland, as the leading exponent of baroque architecture. He designed the palace at Nieborów for Cardinal Radziejowski.

Von Erlach, Johann Bernhard (1656–1723)

Outstanding Austrian-born Baroque architect of the late seventeenth and early eighteenth centuries, who worked on the design of Lednice, Poland.

Von Gontard, Carl (1731–91)

German-born architect of the Marmorpalais at the Neuer Garten, Potsdam.

Von Wittelsbach, Clemens August, elector and archbishop of Cologne (1700–61)

Owner of Augustusburg who commissioned the palace and original garden.

Wallinger, Rosamund (*b. c.*1950)
Owner of the manor house Upton Grey, who carried out the restoration of the Gertrude Jekyll garden.

Washington, George (1732–99)
American soldier and statesman, first president of the United States. Owner of the Mount Vernon estate where he built the house and designed the garden.

Wendland, Johann Christoph (1775–1828) and **Hermann** (1825–1903)
Father and grandson at Herrenhausen, Hanover, who were responsible for the botanic garden there. Hermann was a noted plant-collector.

Wharton, Edith (1862–1937)
American writer, interior designer, and garden designer who made the garden at her home, The Mount, in Massachusetts.

Wilkie, Kim (1955–) English landscape architect who was commissioned to restore the garden of La Pietra.

William of Orange, king of England (1650–1702)
Dutch prince who became king of England and commissioned the palace and garden at Het Loo in the Netherlands. He also extended the palace and gardens at Hampton Court, England.

Wingelmüller, Georg (*c.*1780–1855)
Austrian-born architect who rebuilt the palace at Lednice, Poland.

Zug, Szymon Bogumil (1733–1807)
Leading eighteenth-century Polish garden designer and architect who altered the garden at Nieberów during the late eighteenth century for Michal Hieronim Radziwill and worked extensively for his wife at the neighbouring Arkadia.

Bibliography

PERIODICALS

Country Life
Journal of Garden History

BOOKS

Acton Harold. *Memoirs of an Aesthete* (London: Methuen, 1948 & 1970).

Acton, Harold. *More Memoirs of an Aesthete* (London: Methuen, 1970).

Acton, Harold. *The Villas of Tuscany* (London: Thames and Hudson, 1973).

Attlee, Helena. *Italian Gardens* (London: Frances Lincoln, 2006).

Bowe, Patrick. *Gardens in Central Europe* (New York: Antique Collectors' Club, 1991).

Brinkley, M. Kent, and Chappell, Gordon W. *The Gardens of Colonial Williamsburg* (Williamsburg, VA: Colonial Williamsburg Foundation, 1996).

Buchan, Ursula. *The English Garden* (London: Frances Lincoln, 2006).

Burton, Pamela, and Botnick, Marie. *Private Landscapes* (New York: Princeton Architectural Press, 2002).

Calnan, Mike (ed) *Rooted in History: Studies in Garden Conservation* (London: National Trust Books, 2001).

Casa Valdes, Marquesa de. *Spanish Gardens* (New York: Antique Collectors' Club 1987).

David, Penny. *A Garden Lost in Time: The Mystery of the Ancient Gardens of Aberglasney* (London: Seven Dials, 1999).

Gothein, Marie-Louise. *A History of Garden Art*, 2 vols (London: J M Dent & Sons, 1928)

Hayden, Peter. *Biddulph Grange* (London: National Trust Books, 1989).

Hayden, Peter. *Russian Parks and Gardens* (London: Frances Lincoln, 2005).

Hobhouse, Penelope. *Gardens of Italy* (London: Mitchell Beazley, 1998).

Hobhouse, Penelope, and Taylor, Patrick (eds). *The Gardens of Europe* (London: Random House, 1990).

Jacques, David, and van der Horst, Arend. *The Gardens of William and Mary* (London: Christopher Helm, 1988).

Jellicoe, Geoffrey. *The Landscape of Man* (London: Thames and Hudson, 1975).

Jellicoe, Sir Geoffrey, and Jellicoe, Susan (eds). *The Oxford Companion to Gardens* (Oxford: Oxford University Press, 1986).

Jones, Louisa. *Serre de la Madone* (France: Actes Sud, 2003).

Lacey, Stephen. *Gardens of the National Trust* (London: National Trust Books, 1996).

Laird, Mark. *The Formal Garden* (London: Thames and Hudson, 1992).

Laras, Ann. *Gardens of Italy* (London: Frances Lincoln, 2005).

Lazzaro, Claudia. *The Italian Renaissance Garden* (New Haven: Yale University Press, 1990).

Lévêque, Georges, and Valéry, Marie-Françoise. *French Garden Style* (New York: Barron's Educational Series, 1990).

Longstaffe-Gowan, Todd. *The Gardens and Parks at Hampton Court Palace* (London: Frances Lincoln, 2005).

Masson, Georgina. *Italian Gardens* (New York: Antique Collectors' Club, 1987).

Mosser, Monique, and Teyssot, Georges (eds). *The History of Garden Design* (London: Thames and Hudson, 1991).

Ogrin, Dusan. *The World Heritage of Gardens* (London: Thames and Hudson, 1993).

Page, Russell. *The Education of a Gardener* (London: Random House, 1983).

Perière, Anita, and van Zuylen, Gabrielle. *Private Gardens of France* (London: Weidenfeld and Nicolson, 1983).

Pérouse de Montclos, Jean-Marie. *Vaux le Vicomte* (London: Scala, 1997).

Petherick, Tom. *Heligan: a Portrait of the Lost Gardens* (London: Weidenfeld Nicolson Illustrated, 2004).

Piwkowski, Wlodzimierz. *Arkadia* (Warsaw: 1995).

Piwkowski, Wlodzimierz. *Nieborów* (Warsaw: 2005).

Piwkowski, Wlodzimierz. *The Story of Nieborów* (Warwaw: 2002).

Plumptre, George. *Garden Ornament* (London: Thames and Hudson, 1989).

Plumptre, George. *Royal Gardens of Europe* (London: Mitchell Beazley, 2005).

Plumptre, George. *The Garden Makers* (London: Random House, 1993).

Plumptre, George. *The Water Garden* (London: Thames and Hudson, 1993).

Pool, Mary-Jane. *The Gardens of Florence* (New York: Rizzoli, 1992).

Quest-Ritson, Charles. *Gardens of Germany* (London: Mitchell Beazley, 1998).

Quest-Ritson, Charles. *The English Garden Abroad* (London: Viking, 1992).

Russell, Vivian. *Edith Wharton's Italian Gardens* (London: Frances Lincoln, 1997).

Sales, John. *West Country Gardens* (London: Alan Sutton, 1980).

Smit, Tim. *The Lost Gardens of Heligan* (London: Victor Gollancz, 1997).

Tanner, Ogden. *Gardens of the Hudson River Valley* (New York: Harry N Abrams, 1996).

Taylor, Patrick. *Gardens of Britain* (London: Mitchell Beazley, 1998).

Taylor, Patrick. *Gardens of France* (London: Mitchell Beazley, 1998).

Taylor, Patrick. *The Gardens of Britain and Ireland* (London: DK, 2003).

Taylor, Patrick (ed). *The Oxford Companion to the Garden* (Oxford: Oxford University Press, 2006).

Turner, Richard A. *La Pietra, Florence, a Family and a Villa* (Florence: Edizioni Olivares, 2002).

Wallinger, Rosamund. *Gertrude Jekyll's Lost Garden* (Woodbridge: Garden Art Press, 2000).

Wharton, Edith. *Italian Villas and their Gardens* (London: Century Co., 1904).

Index

Page numbers in **bold** refer to main entries.
Page numbers in *italics* refer to captions.

A

Aberglasney, Camarthenshire, Wales 7, 33,
    56–65
Acton, Arthur 140, 143, 145
Acton, Sir Harold 143–5
Alexander II of Russia 161
Alexander III of Russia 161
Amateur Gardening 151
American Society of Landscape Architects 134
Archbishop of Cologne 18
Arts and Crafts 78, 104
    Upton Grey 10, **124–31**
Atkins, James *21*
Augustusburg, Cologne, Germany 18

B

Baring, Sir Evelyn 52
Baroque
    Herrenhausen **174–81**
    Lednice 70, 74
    Nieborów 165–6, 73
Barry, Sir Charles 73
Barsali, Isa Belli 97, 199
Barton, Coralie 111
Bateman, James and Maria 190, 191
Bernini, Pietro 97
Biddulph Grange, Staffordshire, England **190–2**
Biltmore, USA 107
Bisgrove, Richard 126
Bonaparte, Louis 24
Bonaparte, Napoleon 24
Bonazza, Francesco 143
Bourdeau, Benoît 52
Bridgeman, Charles 7
Brodsworth, Yorkshire, England **76–81**
Brown, Lancelot "Capability" 7, 20, 73
Busch, John 157, 158

C

Caldéron, General Don Carlos 100
Capitol, Washington DC 195
Capponi family 143
Caratti, Francesco 70
Carmen de Los Martires, Spain 11, **98–103**
Carvallo, Dr. Joachim 43, 44
Casentini, G. M. 77
Castellane, Marquis de 43
Castelnaud, France 82, 86
Catherine the Great 156–8
Cecilienhof, Potsdam, Germany 182, 186, 187
Cerval, François de 82–5
Cerval, Julien de 85–6, 88
Charbonnier, Martin 177–8
Charles, John 59
Chasse, Patrick 37
Château d'Harcourt, France 9
Château de Chantilly, France 158, 160
Château de Courances, Ile de France, France
    10–11, 189, **200–1**

Château de Fayrac, France 82
Château de Marqueyssac, France **82–9**
Château de Vaux-le-Vicomte, Seine et Marne,
    France 10–11, 16
Château de Villandry, Tours, France **40–6**, 56
Child, Susan 138
Churchill, Winston 182
Ciolek, Gerard 173
Claremont, Surrey, England 7
Clément, Gilles 52, 53
Codman, Ogden 132
Colchester, Maynard 15
Coleman, Ann 43
Colonial Williamsburg, USA 189, **196–7**
Colvin and Moggridge 63
Compton Wynyates, Warwickshire, England 104
Condé, Prince de 158, 160
Conservatoire du Littoral 46, 52
Cooke, Edward 190
Country Life 52, 77

D

d'Este, Cardinal Ippolito II 199
Daily Mail 146
David, Penny 56–9, 63
Davis, Alexander Jackson 111, 115, 117
Delafield, Violetta 10, 112, 113
Destailleurs, Gabriel Hippolyte 16, 200–1
Devien, P. H. 73
Dickinson, Lord 22
Downing, Andrew Jackson 111, 115, 118
    Landscape Gardening 113
Du Cerceau, Jacques Androuet *Les Plus Excellents
    Bastiments de France* 43
Du Pont family 104
Duca, Giacomo del 92
Duchêne, Achille 16, 143, 201
Dyer, Robert 59

E

East Lambrook Manor, Somerset, England
    146–53
Eden Project 33
Edith Wharton Restoration (EWR) 136–8
Elizabeth I 62
Elizabethan 733
Engel, Johann Karl 73
English Heritage 78–80
English Landscape 7, 18, 20, 43, 67, 143, 176
    Lednice 70
    Neuer Garten 185
Eyserbeck, Johann August 185

F

Falllingwater, Pennsylvania, USA 35
Farnese, Cardinal Alessandro II 92, 94, 97
Farrand, Beatrix 7, 37, 134, 138
Field, The 151
Fish, Margery 146–52
Forrest, George 50
Fouquet, Nicolas 16
François I 40
Frederick the Great of Prussia 182–5
Frederick William II of Prussia 185
Frogmore House, Berkshire, England 81
Fullerton, Morton 134

G

Ganay, Ernest de 9, 48, 52
Ganay, Marquis de 201
Garden Conservancy 7
Garland Farm, Maine USA 37
Gatchina, St Petersburg, Russia **156–63**
George I 178
Girouard, Mark 77, 81
Gontard, Carl 185
Gothic
    Brodsworth 81
Gothick
    Painswick House 22
Gould, Helen and Anna 118
Gould, Jay 117, 118
Grant-Dalton, Mrs 77–8

H

Haber, Baron Samuel de 200
Hackett, James 157
Haddon Hall, Derbyshire 104
Hampshire Gardens Trust 128
Hampton Court, Middlesex, England 22, 25–7
Hanover, Duke Johann Friedrich 174
Hanover, Electress Sophie 174–7
Hardtmuth, Joseph 70
Harris, Dr Walter 24
Harvard University Graduate School of Design 138
Harvey, George 120
Heligan, Cornwall, England 7, 31–3, 34
Herrenhausen, Germany **174–81**
Het Loo, Netherlands 10, 22–5, 27, 177
Hidcote Bartram Manor, Gloucestershire, England
    46, 49, 51, 52
Historic Buildings Council 14
Historic Hudson Valley 112
Hobhouse, Penny 56, *59*, 64, 95, 128
Holle, Ignac 70
Holme, Charles 126
Hudson River Gardens, New York State, USA
    110–21
Hyères, France 48

I

Infantado, Duke del 100
Ingram, Collingwood "Cherry" 50
Ingram, Sir George 50
Irving, Washington 118–21
Isabella I of Spain 100
Italianate
    Brodsworth 78, 81
    Lednice 73, 74
Ittar, Henryk 170

J

James, Henry 138
Jefferson, Thomas 192
Jekyll, Gertrude 7, 10, 78, 123, 124–30, 134
Johnston, Lawrence 7, 10, 46–52, 55
Jones, Louis 55

K

Karl I of Liechtenstein 68
Karl Eusebius II of Liechtenstein 68–70
Kaufmann Desert House, California, USA 34–5,
    36, 37
Kaufmann, Edgar J 35

Kent, William 7
Kerenski, Alexandr 161
Kew Royal Botanical Gardens, England 73, 178
Kip, Johannes 15
Kléber Rossillon 86
Kornhäusel, Joseph 73
Kykuit, USA 121

L

La Majorelle, Morocco 27–8
Latrobe, Benjamin 195
Laves, Georg Ludwig Friedrich 178
Le Breton, Jean 40–3
Le Brun, Charles 16
Le Coeur, Jules 200
Le Nôtre, André 16, 82, 200
Le Nôtre, Jean 200
Le Vau, Louis 16
Lednice and Valtice, Czech Republic 7, **68–75**
Lenin, Vladimir Ilyich 161
Lenné, Peter Joseph 18, 185, 187
Lewis Glyn Cothi 59
Liechtenstein family 68–70, 74
Ligorio, Pirro 199
Lindsay, Nancy 52
Lindsay, Norah 52
Lorentz, Stanislaw 172
Loudon, J. C. 117
Louis XIV 16, 40, 82, 174
Lutyens, Edwin 124
Lvov, Nikolai 160
Lyndhurst, New York State, USA 111, 115–18

M

Majorelle, Jacques 27, 28
Majorelle, Louis 27, 28
Malecki, Bill 191–2
Mangold, Ferdinand 117, 118
Manning, Warren 104, 107–9
Maria Fedorovna, Grand Duchess, 158–61
Marinali, Orazio 143
Marmorpalais, Germany 185
Marot, Daniel 22, 25
Marqueyssac, Bertrand Vernet de 82
Martinelli, Domenico 70
Master of the Tumbled Chairs" 7
Meersmans, Hubert 100
Merritt, George 117
Modernism
    Kaufmann Desert House 34–5, *36, 37*
Moggridge, Hal 63–4
Monasticum Gallicanum 43
Montgomery Place, New York State, USA 10, 110–15
Montgomery, Edward Livingston 111
Montgomery, Janet Livingston 110–11, 113
Mount Vernon Ladies Association 192, 195
Mount Vernon, Virginia, USA 11, **192–5**
Mount, Massachusetts, USA 7, **132–9**
Mowl, Timothy 22
Mughal
    Shalimar Bagh 7, 28–31
Munstead Wood, Surrey, England 128

N

National Register of Historic Places 37, 134–6
National Trust 7, 10, 14, 51, 78, 146, 190–2
National Trust for Historic Preservation 118, 136

neo-Gothic
    Lednice *71*, 73, 74
Neoclassical
    Brodsworth 77
    Gatchina **156–63**
    Lednice 70, 74
Neuer Garten, Potsdam, Germany **182–7**
Neutra, Richard 34–5
New York University 140, 145
Newport, USA 104
Newton, Ernest 126
Nicholas I of Russia 161
Nicholas II of Russia 161
Nicholson, Francis 196
Nieborów and Arkadia, Lowitz, Poland **164–73**
Niemcewicz, Julian 195
Noailles, Charles de 48
Norblin, Jean-Pierre 169
Norton, Andrew 152

O

Olmsted, Frederick Law 107
Orlov, Count Grigory 156–7
Orlowski, Alekxander 169
Osborne House, Isle of Wight , England 78

P

Paddock, William *107*
Painswick House, Gloucestershire, England 20–2
Parc André Citroën, Paris 52
Paul I of Russia 157–60
Paul III, Pope 92
Paulding, William 115
Pavlovsk, Russia 160, 162
Peruzzi, Baldassare 92
Peter III of Russia 156
Peter the Great of Russia 11, 13, 156, 157
Peterhof, St Petersburg, Russia 11–13, 14, 156, 162
Phillips, Thomas 59
Piranesi, Giovanni Batista 170
Pius X, Pope 86
planting 10
    Aberglasney 64
    Brodsworth 78–81
    Carmen de Los Martires 100
    Château de Marqueyssac 85–8
    Château de Villandry 43–4
    Serre de la Madone 48–51
    Upton Grey 128–30
Pococke, Bishop 22
Poe, Edgar Allan 191
Portland, Duchess of 80
Poussin, Nicolas 169
Powkowski, Wlodzimierz 170

R

Radziejowski, Cardinal 165
Radziner, Marmol 35
Radziwill, Helena 166–9, 170, 172, 173
Radziwill, Janusz 172
Radziwill, Michal Hieronim 165–6, 172
Rainaldi, Girolamo 92, 97
Reef Point Gardens Collection, University of
        California 126
Renaissance
    Château de Villandry **40–6**, 56
    Villa Farnese **92–7**

Villa la Pietra **140–5**
Renoir, Auguste 200
Rhydderch ap Rhys 59
Rinaldi, Antonio 157
Robins, Thomas 22
Robinson, William 78
Rockefeller, John D. Jr. 121, 196
Rococo
    Painswick House 20–2
Roman, Jacob 22
Romantic
    Arkadia 166–73
    Lednice 70, 74
Roseraie de l'Haÿ-les-Roses, France 130
Rousseau, Jean-Jacques 170
Royal Institute of British Architects 126
Rudd, Anthony 59

S

Saint Laurent, Yves 28
Sales, John 14–15, 146–9
Sangallo, Antonio da 92
Sanssouci, Germany 182–5
Sartorio, Hieronomo 174
Sassetti, Francesco 143
Save America's Treasures (SAT) 138
Schneider, Charles S. 104
Schönbrunn, Vienna, Austria 70
Seiberling family 109
Seiberling, Franklin A. 104
Seiberling, Gertrude 104, 107–8
Serre de la Madone, Menton, France 7, 10, 33,
        46–55, 56
Shah Jahan 29
Shalimar Bagh, Lahore, Pakistan 7, **28–31**
Shipman, Ellen Biddle 108
Shulman, Julius 35
Shurcliff, Arthur 196
Sierakowski, Josef 169
Simonov, Vasily 13
Sintra, Portugal 74
Sisley, Alfred 200
Smit, Tim 31–3
Smith, William Loughton 195
Sommier, Alfred 16
Sparrow, James 157
Staggi, Gioacchino 169, 173
Stalin, Josef 182
Stan Hywet Hall, Ohio, USA 10, **104–9**
statuary 13, 16, 92–4, 95–7, 143, 169, 180
Stourhead, England 169
Stowe, England 169
Suarez, Diego 143
Sunnyside, New York State, USA 120–1
Sutton Courtenay, Oxfordshire, England 52

T

Taj Mahal, Agra 29
Taylor, Peter 33
Tencalla, Giovanni Giacomo 70
Thellusson, Charles 77
Thomas, Graham Stuart 7
Tijou, Jean 25, 27
Tikhomirova, Marina 13
Trentham, Staffordshire, England 73, 78
Truman, Harry 182
Tsarskoye Selo, Russia 157, 162

U

Uebelacher, Joseph 70
UNESCO 7, 28, 31, 68, 74, 187
Upton Grey, Hampshire, England 10, **124–31**

V

Van Asbeck, J. B. 24–5
Van Der Schott, Joseph 70
Van Gameren, Tylman 165
Van Staden, Christiaan Pieter 24
Vanbrugh, Sir John 7
Vasari, Giorgio the Younger 143
Vaughan, Samuel 195
Versailles, France 16, 74, 82, 174
Victor Emmanuel of Italy 97
Victoria 81, 186
Victorian style 67
    Biddulph Grange **190–2**
    Brodsworth 81
Vignola, Giacomo Barozzi da 92, 94, 97
Villa d'Este, Tivoli, Italy 11, 97, **198–9**
Villa Farnese, Caprarola, Italy **92–7**
Villa la Pietra, Italy **140–5**

Villa Lante, Italy 94
Virgil 166–9
Vizcaya, Florida, USA 143
Von Erlach, Johann Bernard Fischer 70

W

Wallinger, Rosamund and John 10, 124, 126–30
Walter, John William 117
Washington, George 11, 118, 119, 192–5
water gardens
    Carmen de Los Martires 100–2
    Château de Courances 200–1
    Château de Vaux-le-Vicomte 16
    Herrenhausen 177–8, 180
    Villa d'Este *199*
    Villa Farnese *93*, 95
    Westbury Court 14–15
Wendland, Hermann 178
Wendland, Johann Christoph 178
Westbury Court, Gloucestershire, England 10, 14–15, 16
Wharton, Edith 48, 97, 132–4, 138
White, Roger 22

White, Stanford 140
Whiting, Anthony 195
Whitsey, Fred 52
Whitty, Maureen 152
Wilhelmina of Holland 24
Wilkie, Kim 145
Wilkinson, Philip 77
William II of Germany 186
William of Orange 22, 24, 25
Williams, Robin and Marianne 152
Windsor Castle, Berkshire, England 81
Wingelmüller, Georg 73
Winthrop, Gertrude 46
World Heritage Sites 7, 28, 68, 74, 187, 199
Wren, Sir Christopher 25
Würstemburger, Jacques de 52

Z

Zug, Szymon Bogumil 165–6, 169, 173

Acknowledgments

The author would like to acknowledge the assistance of Ruth Chivers in the preparation of entries for gardens in the United States.

Mitchell Beazley would like to acknowledge and thank all the photographers, agencies, and heritage gardens themselves who have kindly provided material for publication in this book.

2–3 Alamy/A M Corporation; 4–5 John Glover/East Lambrook Manor; 6 Janusz Moniatowicz; 8–9 Photolibrary Group/Ellen Rooney; 10 Alamy/Art Kowalsky; 11, 12–13 Jean-Pierre Gabriel; 14 Harpur Garden Library/Jerry Harpur; 15 Hugh Palmer; 16 Photos12.com/Stéphane Pons; 17 Harpur Garden Library/Jerry Harpur; 18, 19 Alamy/Bildarchiv Monheim GmbH; 20a, 21a and b Clive Nichols; 20b Photolibrary Group/Christopher Gallagher; 22 Harpur Garden Library/Jerry Harpur; 23a Corbis/Nathan Benn; 23b Corbis/Nicolas Sapieha; 24 Clive Nichols; 25 Photolibrary Group/Rex Butcher; 26 Alamy/Skyscan Photolibrary; 27 Robert Harding/Peter Higgins; 28, 29 Photolibrary Group/Clay Perry; 30 Getty Images/Hulton Archive; 31 Alamy/Tibor Bognar; 32a and b Harpur Garden Library/Jerry Harpur/Heligan, Cornwall; 33 John Glover; 34a and b, 35, 36 Tim Street-Porter; 37 Corbis/Arcaid/Alan Weintraub; 38–9 Alamy/Tom Mackie; 40 Photolibrary Group/Photononstop/Brigitte Merle; 41 Clive Nichols; 42a Harpur Garden Library/Jerry Harpur/Villandry; 42b TopFoto/Alinari; 43 The Garden Collection/Liz Eddison; 44 Photolibrary Group/Erika Craddock; 45 Garden Collection/Liz Eddison; 46 Harpur Garden Library/Jerry Harpur/Serre de La Madone; 47 Le Scanff/Mayer; 48a Vivian Russell; 48b courtesy of Ville de Menton; 49, 50 LeScanff/Mayer; 51 Map/Mise au Point/Alain Kubacsi; 52, 53 Le Scanff/Mayer; 54, 55 Harpur Garden Library/Jerry Harpur; 56–65 all courtesy of Aberglasney, Camarthenshire, with the exception of 59, Photolibrary Wales/Kathy de Witt; 66–7 Camera Press/Gamma/Raphael Gaillarde; 68 www.lednice.cz; 69 Bilderberg/Berthold Steinhilber; 70 Alamy/Petr Svarc; 71, 72l Alamy/Isifa Image Service rso; 72r www.lednice.cz; 73 Bilderberg/Andrej Reiser; 74 Camera Press/Isafa/Tomas Kubes; 75 Robert Harding/Ken Gillham; 76 English Heritage Photo Library/John Critchley; 77 courtesy Brodsworth Hall; 78–9 English Heritage Photo Library/Nigel Corrie; 80 English Heritage Photolibrary/Bob Skingle; 81a courtesy Brodsworth Hall; 81b English Heritage Photo Library/Paul Highnam; 82 courtesy Jardins de Marqueyssac/Laugery; 83 Yann Monel; 84–5 Jean-Pierre Gabriel; 86a and b, 87 Yann Monel; 88, 89 Anzenberger/Jarry-Tripelon; 90–1 Photolibrary Group/John Ferro Sims; 92 Art Archive/Dagli Orti; 93 akg-images/Jürgen Sorges; 94 Hugh Palmer; 95 Corbis/Sandro Vannini; 96, 97 Vivian Russell; 98 Foto Alinari; 99 Narratives/Quick Image/David Gavin; 100 Hugh Palmer;

101 Superstock/Jean Dominique Dallet; 102, 103 Narratives/Quick Image/David Gavin; 104–8 all courtesy Stan Hywet Hall and Gardens; 109 Harpur Garden Library/Jerry Harpur; 110–15 all courtesy Historic Hudson Valley, Tarrytown, NY; 116 IPN Stock/Gabe Palacio; 117 courtesy Lyndhurst/James Bleecker; 118, 119b Lyndhurst/Jim Frank; 119a Lyndhurst 120 courtesy Historic Hudson Valley, Tarrytown, NY/Bryan Haeffele; 121a and b Dency Kane; 122–3 courtesy The Mount Estate and Gardens, Lenox, MA; 124 Country Life Picture Library; 125 John Glover; 126 Andrew Lawson; 127a Environmental Design Archives, University of California, Berkeley; 127b Harpur Garden Library/Marcus Harpur; 128 Environmental Design Archives, University of California, Berkeley; 129, 130a and b, 131 Harpur Garden Library/Marcus Harpur; 132–9 all courtesy The Mount Estate and Gardens, Lenox, MA, with the exception of 134, akg-images, 137a courtesy of The Lenox Library Association, Lenox, MA; 140, 141 Alex Ramsay; 142a Vivian Russell; 142b Foto Alinari; 143 Corbis/George W Wright; 144, 145a and b Alex Ramsay; 146 courtesy East Lambrook Manor Gardens, photo by Valerie Finnis; 147, 148 Harpur Garden Library/Marcus Harpur; 149a Andrew Lawson; 149b Mark Bolton; 150 Harpur Garden Library/Marcus Harpur; 151, 152 John Glover; 153 Mark Bolton; 154–5 H & Z Bildagentur/Corbis Sygma; 156–63 all Galina Puntusova, http://history.gatchina.ru, with the exception of 161a and 162a, Gatchina Palace and Museum, courtesy Galina Puntusova; 164–73 all Janusz Moniatowicz, with the exception of 165a Nieborow Palace Museum courtesy Janusz Moniatowicz, 165b courtesy of Nieborow Palace Museum; 174–5 Alamy/blickwinckel; 176a akg-images; 176b Hugh Palmer; 177 akg-images/Reimer Wulf; 178 akg-images/Jost Schilgen; 179 Alamy/Bilarchiv Monheim GmbH; 180 Bildarchiv Monheim; 181a Getty Images/Photographer's Choice/Werner Dieterich; 181b The Bridgeman Art Library/Stapleton Collection/Private Collection; 182 ArchivBerlin; 183 akg images/Ullstein Bild; 184 Archiv Berlin/U Boettcher, 185a and b Archiv Berlin; 186 akg-images; 187 Alamy/John Stark; 188–9 Harpur Garden Library/Jerry Harpur; 190 National Trust Photo Library/Andrew Butler; 19 Garden World Images; 193 National Trust Photolibrary/Andrew Butler; 194 and b Mount Vernon Estate and Gardens, Washington DC, Mount Vernon Ladies' Association; 195 Alamy/George and Monserrate Schwartz; 196–7 Getty Images/Panoramic Images; 197a Harpur Garden Library/Jerry Harpur; 198 Getty Images/Robert Harding/Nedra Westwater; 199 Alamy/Peter Barritt.